Parenting under pressure

Parenting under pressure

Mothers and fathers with learning difficulties

TIM BOOTH
WENDY BOOTH

Open University Press
Buckingham · Philadelphia

Open University Press
Celtic Court
22 Ballmoor
Buckingham
MK18 1XW

and
1900 Frost Road, Suite 101
Bristol, PA 19007, USA

First Published 1994

A catalogue record of this book is available from the British Library

ISBN 0 335 19194 0 (pbk)   0 335 19269 6 (hbk)

Library of Congress Cataloging-in-Publication Data
Booth, Timothy A., 1947–
    Parenting under pressure : mothers and fathers with learning difficulties / Tim Booth, Wendy Booth.
        p.   cm.
    Includes bibliographical references and index.
    ISBN 0–335–19269–6   ISBN 0–335–19194–0 (pbk.)
    1. Handicapped parents–Great Britain–Case studies. 2. Learning disabled–Great Britain–Case studies. I. Booth, Wendy, 1946–   . II. Title.
HQ759.912.B66 1994
306.874–dc20

                                                                          94–230
                                                                          CIP

Typeset by Type Study, Scarborough
Printed in Great Britain by St Edmundsbury Press, Bury St Edmunds, Suffolk

At that Mother got proper blazing,
    'And thank you, sir, kindly,' said she,
'What waste all our lives raising children
To feed ruddy Lions? Not me!'
                    (Marriott Edgar, 1932)

Contents

Acknowledgements

Where to begin? So many people, so many debts.

First and foremost our thanks go to the Nuffield Foundation, which funded both our research and a Social Science Fellowship for Tim Booth to assist the writing of this book. In particular, we are grateful to Pat Thomas for her friendly and efficient support throughout.

Our special thanks are due to Linda Ward and Ann Craft. The study would probably not have got off the ground without their early help and encouragement and several times since we have unashamedly tested their patience and expertise.

We are indebted to the help we received during the course of our fieldwork from practitioners and others in Kirklees, Wakefield and Sheffield. They must remain anonymous but we are happy to express our thanks publicly.

Our Reference Group, set up to provide a sounding board for ideas and a backstop on sensitive ethical issues, gave us valuable service as well as providing a sense of security. We are grateful to Michael Bayley, Harold Loxley, Julie Gosling, Sue MacMahon, and Brian Mettrick for their time and effort.

Others who gave us a lift on the way include: Alastair Allan, Jan Walmsley, Terry Philpot, Gwynnyth Llewellyn, Jeremy Pritlove, Chris Melotte, Fred Sykes, Bob Thomas, Jane Padget, the Elfrida Rathbone 'Women as Parents' Group, and members of Huddersfield People First.

The University of Sheffield Research Fund and the British Academy generously awarded us travel grants to attend the Third International People First Conference in Toronto.

We should also like to thank the editors of the following journals for permission to draw on material originally published by them: *British Journal of Social Work*; *Health and Social Care in the Community*; *Disability and*

Society; Social Work and Social Sciences Review; Mental Handicap and *Social Science and Medicine*.

Jill Kerkhoff has managed the office with her usual quiet assurance and skill.

It is difficult to thank the parents who took part in the study without sounding trite. We do so humbly.

CHAPTER 1

Introduction

This book is about the experience of childrearing and parenthood as recounted by mothers and fathers with learning difficulties. Very little is known about the lives and struggles of these parents. What information we have refers more to their problems than to them as people. Our aim is to put right this omission by giving pride of place to the views of parents themselves and what they have to say about the rewards and demands of parenthood. By using the life story approach as 'an antidote to accounts which come from other quarters' (Atkinson and Williams 1990), we hope to provide an insight into what it means to be a parent with learning difficulties that will act as a counterweight to research in which the parents as people make no appearance. This approach is based on the view, shared with Thompson (1981), that, because parenting and the bringing up of children are essentially private and domestic matters, the sensitive life story 'offers almost the only way towards understanding and interpreting them'.

A study of parenting offers a new angle of vision on a number of important, contemporary issues and raises searching questions about the assumptions that underpin current thinking about the needs and rights of people with learning difficulties:

- *Normalization*: How far is the principle that people should be enabled to enjoy 'the same rights, responsibilities and opportunities as are available to others' (Perrin and Nirje 1985) applied to parenthood? Are people supported in making this choice? If not, what more should be done?
- *An 'ordinary life'*: Since it was first coined, the term an 'ordinary life' has changed from a description of a model residential service to 'a shorthand way of symbolising the philosophy which should guide the provision of services' (Towell 1982). One of the fundamental principles underlying

this philosophy is that people with learning difficulties have a right and a need to live like others in the community. For most people an ordinary life means marriage and children. How can we reduce the obstacles and problems facing people with learning difficulties who try to live up to these aspirations?

- *Community care*: The control exercised over people's sexuality and fertility is greater and more invasive in institutional settings. Community care ought to bring comparatively more personal freedom. In this context, knowing what kind of education, counselling and support should be provided to help people manage their personal relationships and make responsible choices, and what constitutes good practice in this field, becomes more urgent.

- *Human rights and citizenship*: The United Nation's Declaration of the Rights of Mentally Retarded Persons declares that people with learning difficulties have 'the same basic rights as other citizens of the same country and the same age'. This is normally interpreted as embodying the right to any additional help they may need in order to claim their common rights as citizens. Is it realistic to recognize the right of procreation for people with learning difficulties, and what limits might have to be placed on the additional help needed to secure this right? Equally, how should the power of statutory authorities to prevent mothers and fathers with learning difficulties fulfilling their role as parents be restricted?

- *'Good parenting'*: The notion of 'fitness for parenthood' is often invoked as a criterion for denying people with learning difficulties the choice of bearing or rearing children of their own. How do the standards of good parenting applied by professionals match up to those of the parents themselves?

- *Social justice and discrimination*: Should the right to parenthood be withheld from people with learning difficulties simply because they might fail to achieve or maintain standards of childrearing that are not even imposed as a prior condition on other people? What sort of discriminatory attitudes and actions do parents with learning difficulties encounter among professionals and the public at large?

This study was not designed to answer all these questions. Our small hope is that it will add purchase to our grasp of the issues, enhance our understanding of their ramifications, and represent the views and experiences of parents themselves whose own voice has been conspicuously absent from the literature in this field.

The study design was chosen to provide a parent's view of parenting using the life story approach. The purpose is not generalization. There is no sampling frame for this group of parents. The life story approach of depth interviewing is intensive, time-consuming and precludes a large sample. As Erikson (1973) says, sampling is 'a strategy of plenty'; doing life stories demands a more frugal approach. Consequently, we set out to produce personal accounts that are typical, if not strictly representative, of parents with learning difficulties. By looking for the common threads in their lives we aimed to use these stories in a way that is true to the experience of such parents at the level of subjective reality rather than statistical description.

Parents were mostly located through health and social services agencies using the 'key informant' method, although a few were traced from grapevine information picked up in the course of fieldwork from other contacts and study families. Identifying, tracing and contacting parents with learning difficulties is a major logistical challenge and a fundamental obstacle to epidemiological or survey-type research. Almost all statistical studies to date can be criticized on methodological grounds for selection bias. Locating parents through service agencies and similar formal chan-nels risks skewing the study towards people with problems and so unwittingly reinforcing a presumption of parental inadequacy. This is the reason why the sensitive life story, aimed at generating insights rather than generalizations, is ideally suited to the task at hand. Anyway, we were interested primarily in parents whose learning difficulties were such as to make it unlikely that they could manage without outside support. Unlike people with milder learning difficulties, who often merge into the wider population once they leave school, this group usually experience problems in living, certainly after having children, that bring them into contact with the statutory authorities.

A 'social systems perspective' (Mercer 1973) was adopted as the main diagnostic criterion for determining whether parents were eligible for admission to the study on account of their learning difficulties. Parents were considered admissible if one or both partners at some time in their lives, not necessarily currently, had been in receipt of specialist services specifically intended for people with learning difficulties. These included mental handicap hospitals, special schools, adult training centres, social education centres, health and local authority hostels and similar voluntary or private accommodation. This same criterion is used by many health authorities for defining the people who are eligible for registration with mental handicap case registers (Farmer et al., 1993). Although the approach has obvious limitations, it is the most satisfactory way of dealing with the absence of test data in most cases and with the abandonment by many professional workers of the use of IQ as a classificatory device (Budd and Greenspan 1984).

The study comprised a two-stage design. The first stage involved unstructured interviews with 20 parents or sets of parents in different circumstances aimed at providing comparable information on their experiences of parenthood from becoming pregnant, through pregnancy, confinement and labour, to baby care, childrearing and being a mother or father. The second stage involved the compilation of in-depth personal accounts of people's ongoing situation as parents. Six couples and one single mother were selected from the first stage to go forward into this part of the study. As Plummer (1983) has stressed, 'biographies are in a constant state of becoming' and the guiding purpose of this stage of the research was to capture something of this ebb and flow of experience by presenting a picture of a 'year in the life' of these families. To the extent that every biographical account reconstructs the meaning of the past from the present point of view (Bertaux-Wiame 1981), our task involved understanding people's lives in the here-and-now in order to gain a better insight into their own life stories.

Contact with these families has been extensive: 126 interviews were conducted as part of the study between July 1991 and December 1992. In addition, links were maintained by phone calls (121), brief social calls (15), and trips and outings with parents (22). We have also attended case reviews, parties, a Family Centre and Women's Group, visited people in hospital, attended a DSS interview and a court appearance, and dropped in on people at their Social Education Centre. Involvement has been more intensive with some families than others. The minimum level of involvement with a single family in the first stage of the study was one depth interview and the maximum was six interviews (plus phone calls, outings and other visits). In the second stage the minimum was nine interviews and the maximum was 20 (excluding other forms of contact).

A total of 33 parents (20 mothers and 13 fathers) took part in the study of whom 25 (18 mothers and 7 fathers) had learning difficulties. There were five couples where both partners had learning difficulties.

At the beginning there were eight married couples in the study, three long-standing unmarried partnerships, five single parents (four mothers), four divorced mothers and one separated couple. Between them these parents had a total of 50 children, of whom two were married (one with children of their own), 26 lived at home with their parents, four with an ex-partner outside the study, one with grandparents, five had been adopted, eight fostered, one was originally placed in temporary care but subsequently returned home, one had been killed in a road accident, one lived independently, and one child was untraceable.

Just over half (26) of these 50 children belonged to partnerships in the study; the remaining 24 either came from relationships that had ended or from casual or forced sexual encounters including rape (in three cases) and incest (one). The reported incidence of physical or sexual abuse suffered by the parents themselves either as children or later in adult life was high: 14 parents (including 13 of the 20 mothers) acknowledged having experienced some form of abuse other than corporal punishment in their lives. In turn, firm evidence was found in five cases of study parents (three with learning difficulties) having abused their own children.

At the start of the study, most (14) of the 20 families were living in rented council accommodation. Of the rest, two were owner-occupiers, two lived with their own parents (including one couple living separately in their respective parental homes), one couple lived in a caravan, and one divorced parent lived in a social services hostel. For the parents as a whole, their housing conditions mirrored the poverty of resources that cramped the rest of their lives. Only two parents were in full-time, paid employment.

This summary description of the parents and their families presents a static picture of a moving scene. In the course of the study, some parents split up (two married couples), some got together again (two couples) and others entered new relationships (four). Similarly, one child left home and two were taken into care, while one was reunited with her family. To date, 13 people have moved house since they were first contacted. Seven more are currently wanting to move: in some cases to escape victimization by neighbours. Fully 12 of the 20 families reported having experienced harassment from outsiders. Research through time is rendered more complex in the telling by the simple fact that people's lives do not stand still.

Following the distinction drawn by Bertaux (1981), we set out to collect life stories of our subjects rather than compile their life histories. A life story is an account of all or part of someone's life delivered orally by that person. A life history subsumes the life story but also includes biographical information from a range of other sources. The life history is widely considered to be methodologically more rigorous because it allows for the cross-checking of information and the triangulation of data. We are not convinced of the validity of this point in our study. Where the parents were living together (in just over half our cases) it was possible to check the accuracy of matters of fact with the other partner in the couple. Also, as our involvement with families usually stretched over several interviews, it was possible to check for consistency by revisiting topics and repeating questions on separate occasions. Lastly, we share the view that insight into how people grasp their own subjective world only comes via the experience of the active human subject – in our case, the parents themselves. Beyond these issues, however, another consideration influenced our decision to adopt a life story approach.

The research literature in this field has disregarded the perspective of parents. Most evidence comes from expert, official, clinical or professional sources. This illustrates what Becker (1967) has called the 'hierarchy of credibility' which gives people with power and status 'the right to define the way things really are'. In any system of ranks where credibility and the right to be heard are not equally distributed, the voice of those at the top tends to prevail. In other words, there is an in-built bias within the system which accords greater weight and legitimacy to the views of certain people. Those who occupy important positions are also vested with moral authority: they are presumed to know best.

Conversely, people in subordinate groups are presumed to lack cognizance and their interpretations of reality are denied authenticity (Young 1969). A survey of the literature lends support to the view that this bias has operated to give undue prominence to the judgements and perceptions of professionals in research on parents with learning difficulties. Part of the purpose of our study is to rectify this balance in some small way by giving priority and moral precedence to the accounts of parents. Sometimes it is necessary to drive a wedge between lay and professional views, or between the individual and the institutions of the state, in order to see more clearly what the latter are doing, especially to people as vulnerable as the parents in our study whose existence is widely seen as a threat to family values and the moral order.

Our concern is not with theorizing but with harnessing for practical ends what can be learned from listening to parents. This book seeks to bring research and practice into closer alignment by framing a set of 'good practice' guidelines grounded on parents' perceptions of their own needs in order to assist practitioners and service providers in developing a clearer view of their task. First, however, let us examine the lessons for practice and support within the wider research literature.

CHAPTER 2

Research, practice and parenting

The true prevalence of parents with learning difficulties is unknown and possibly unknowable. At the moment, as Whitman et al. (1986) have observed, they represent 'an invisible and underserved special-needs population.' Most researchers agree, however, that their number is steadily growing as a result of deinstitutionalization, decreased segregation, changing attitudes towards sexuality and wider opportunities for independent living and participation in the community (Haavik and Menninger 1981; Rosenberg and McTate 1982; Attard 1988). This trend calls for recognition in the planning and delivery of services. Professionals have yet to face up to the practice implications of this aspect of community care policy. In 1991, for example, Lancashire County Council was censured by the Local Government Ombudsman for maladministration in failing to provide the level of counselling and support needed by a mother with learning difficulties. The Ombudsman recommended that the Council 'need to ensure that their social workers have a clearer view of what their aims are at any one time when working with such clients' (Local Government Ombudsman 1991). Too little practical guidance is currently available to help front-line workers decide how best they can secure and uphold the citizenship rights of these parents as well as protect the welfare of their children. In this chapter, we set out to review some of the main practice principles that emerge from the research literature on parents with learning difficulties.

The extent of parenting

There are no reliable estimates of the numbers of parents with learning difficulties. Moreover, the methodological obstacles to undertaking a sound epidemiological study in the community seem to be insurmountable (Whitman and Accardo 1990). What evidence there is about the extent of childbearing among people with learning difficulties comes mostly from follow-up studies of formerly institutionalized populations or from administrative censuses of official records (Brandon 1960; Shaw and Wright 1960; Laxova et al. 1973; Scally 1973; Berg and Nyland 1975; Floor et al. 1975; Whitman et al. 1986). Data from these studies are best regarded as indicative only and should be interpreted with caution. Their comparability suffers from variations and changes in the definition of learning difficulties both over time and cross-nationally (Greenspan and Budd 1986; Gath 1988). This problem is compounded by inconsistencies in the use of terminology (Tymchuk 1990b). Also, they undoubtedly underestimate the extent of parenthood because of the undernotification of fathers. Nevertheless, for all these limitations, they do support a few summary points.

First, the research shows there are significant numbers of adults with learning difficulties in the community who are parents. Shaw and Wright (1960) identified 242 married people from the 2,877 case records of all people since 1915 formally ascertained as having learning difficulties in Sheffield. Of this number, 197 people were eventually traced and found to have produced a total of 377 children. In a similar fashion, Scally (1973) examined the case records of all 4,631 people with learning difficulties known to the public authorities in Northern Ireland, and identified 342 people who were married or who had had at least one pregnancy (32 men and 310 women, representing 10 per cent of all people with learning difficulties over the age of 16). Among this group, Scally counted a total of 887 pregnancies leading to 791 live births. More recently, Whitman et al. (1986) reported the results of a community-based survey of the number of parents with learning difficulties known to agencies providing services in the city of St Louis. They found 402 referred parents of 1,096 children. Parenthood may be seen as both a choice and a consequence of ordinary living. With the continuing spread of 'ordinary life' principles as the basis for service delivery (King's Fund Centre 1980) the number of parents can be expected to rise (Gillberg and Geijer-Karlsson 1983).

Second, the research demonstrates that when people with learning difficulties are freed from invasive control over their sexuality more of them will have children. The old public institutions were built precisely for the purpose of preventing reproduction (Bass 1963–64). Segregation of the sexes and isolation from the world outside were responses to eugenic fears about the supposed threat to the national gene pool posed by the fecundity of the mentally unfit. Of course, sex could not be suppressed by high walls or locked wards. Inmates might be deprived of their liberty, but intimacy was not so easily denied. Same-sex friendships were common, but also a considerable number of children were conceived and born in hospital.

Laxova et al. (1973), for example, report that conception was known to have taken place during admission in 28 of the 96 pregnancies recorded among 53 (5.3 per cent) of the 991 women admitted to Harperbury Hospital between 1961 and 1971. Freed from institutional controls, however, the incidence of childbearing increases. Brandon (1960) surveyed 200 women discharged from the Fountain Hospital between 1922 and 1958 and found that 70 of them had given birth to a total of 160 children. Similarly, Floor et al. (1975) followed up 214 former hospital residents now living independently in the community and found that 80 had subsequently married, forming 54 couples with 32 known children between them. Deinstitutionalization, greater independence and decreased segregation widen the opportunities for people to form personal relationships, to meet a partner, to fall in love, to live together, to get married and to start a family (Attard 1988).

Third, the evidence shows that parenting by people with learning difficulties is not a new phenomenon and probably was more widespread in the past than has ever been officially recognized or acknowledged. In his Colchester survey, Penrose (1938) investigated 1,280 patients under the care of the Royal Eastern Counties Institution and found that 67 of the 570 women had produced a total of 124 children. Again, in the first complete tabulation of the Rhode Island Mental Deficiency Register, Wunsch (1951) reports that 886 of the 6,676 people on the register, or 17.9 per cent of those aged 20 and over, were recorded as having children (of whom almost twice as many were mothers as fathers because illegitimate children were reported for women only). Any increase on this historical base as a result of changes in attitudes and policies now under way will add yet more urgency to the already pressing need for service providers, practitioners and professionals to develop forms of education, training and support for parents with learning difficulties.

Research on parenting

There has been scant research on parents with learning difficulties (Feldman 1986). Most is American in origin: there have been fewer than a dozen reported British studies in the past thirty years. The work that has been done has focused on just four main areas of investigation (Tymchuk et al. 1987): issues of heredity and familial handicap; fertility and family size; parental competence and parenting training; and child maltreatment or abuse.

This limited body of research displays many weaknesses. The parents who have been reported on have not been representative. Most have come from an institutional background and have lacked adequate social supports in the community (Feldman 1986). Consequently, they have generally had little experience of family life or of parenting models on which to base their own behaviour (Gath 1988). They have usually been drawn from those known to the services, often the child protection agencies, precisely because they were experiencing serious difficulties of one sort or another (Andron and Tymchuk 1987). Also, virtually all the information currently available refers to mothers only; the role of fathers, with or without learning difficulties, has been neglected (Llewellyn 1990). Indeed, most research has focused on the problems and failings of parents without giving due attention to their competencies and the more positive side of their experience (Greenspan and Budd 1986; Tymchuk and Keltner n.d.). Moreover, the concept of parental adequacy is generally not clearly defined (Dowdney and Skuse 1993) and parents are assessed against implicit middle class standards on the basis of little more than anecdotal evidence about their abilities (Tymchuk 1990b). This failing is compounded when, as has often been the case, no attempt is made to separate the effects on family life of social class, poverty and deprivation from the intellectual limitations of the parent(s) (Brantlinger 1988). Finally, research so far has signally failed to listen to the parents themselves and to represent their own views and experiences of the rewards and demands of parenthood.

For all these reasons, it would be a mistake to assume that research to date presents a true account of the limitations and potential of parents with learning difficulties. It must be borne in mind that our understanding is confined to people who were born, brought up, have lived and had their children during a time of repressive treatment and pervasive discrimination. As Andron and Tymchuk (1987) observe, we may have to wait until a whole generation of people has lived in the community with adequate supports before we can begin fully to appreciate their qualities as parents.

Despite these shortcomings, the research yields enough evidence to challenge many common misapprehensions about parents with learning difficulties and to assist practitioners in developing a clearer view of their aims and approach when working with these families. In the rest of this chapter, we draw on this body of research to identify the key lessons it holds for practice, training and service provision.

Research and practice

Research point 1:   There is no clear relationship between parental competence and intelligence.

On this point the research evidence is consistent and persuasive

(Mickelson 1949; Brandon 1957; Shaw and Wright 1960; Galliher 1973; Mira and Roddy 1980; Schilling et al. 1982). A fixed level of intellectual functioning is neither necessary nor sufficient for adequate parenting and the ability of a parent to provide good-enough child care is not predictable on the basis of intelligence alone (Rosenberg and McTate 1982; Whitman et al. 1989). Parenting behaviour rather than IQ should be the criterion by which parental competence is assessed (Budd and Greenspan 1985).

The practice implications of these findings are that practitioners must:

• beware of the presumption of incompetence that can lead them into focusing exclusively on people's deficiencies, ignoring their capacities and seeing only such evidence as supports their preconceptions;
• avoid what might be called the mistake of false attribution – of seeing all the problems parents may be having entirely in terms of their learning difficulties;
• be wary of making discriminatory judgements about parents with learning difficulties as a group or class: parental competence can only be assessed on a case-by-case basis;
• approach each case with an open mind to allow a balanced assessment of parental adequacy;
• always remember that love and affection are not related to IQ.

Research point 2: There is no agreed standard for defining what constitutes adequate parenting.

'Good parenting' is a vague concept in need of more precise definition (Brantlinger 1988). Although there is a reasonable consensus on the specific dimensions of parenting that are important for child development (Dowdney et al. 1985), there is no agreement on what constitute minimal acceptable standards of good-enough child care. While children are known to need care, supervision, nurture and stimulation, the minimal requirements defining parental competence in these skills are unspecified. Moreover, there is a clear discrepancy between parent and professional perspectives of parental adequacy (Llewellyn 1991; Walton-Allen and Feldman 1991). As Zetlin et al. (1985) have pointed out, the extended family also has its own standards of adequacy 'based on personal, cultural, and social class experience rather than some general normative criteria'. This lack of consensus about ways of assessing the quality of parenting leads practitioners and researchers alike into relying on their own subjective judgements when making decisions. It can result in variations and inconsistencies between different observers and between different types of parent. According to Payne (1978), for example, parents with learning difficulties are more likely to be judged inadequate and deprived of their parental rights than homosexual parents, incarcerated parents or parents with mental health problems, and Czukar (1983) similarly argues that parents with labels have to meet higher expectations than others. It also puts parents who come under professional scrutiny in the position of not knowing how they will be judged, and striving to meet standards that are never made explicit (Painz 1993).

Parental competence is not just a matter of possessing adequate parenting skills. It is also an attributed status which owes as much to the decisions of professionals and the courts as to the behaviour of parents. It is situationally determined by the quality or poverty of the environment in which people live. It is socially constructed in terms of the standards and judgements enforced by the wider society, official agencies and their front-line representatives. People with learning difficulties frequently fall victim to an expectation of parental inadequacy made real through the decisions and actions of those with the power to intervene in their lives.

Practitioners must take note of these problems and:

- work together and with parents to explore the meaning of adequate parenting;
- ensure the standards against which parents are assessed are made explicit to them;
- avoid making value-laden judgements about the adequacy of parenting on the basis of unfair comparisons with middle class standards;
- pay equal regard to people's parenting skills as well as their deficits;
- watch out for self-fulfilling prophecies of parenting failure based on single-minded concern only with parental inadequacies.

Research point 3:   It is important to distinguish the effects of environmental pressures on parental competence from the effects of having learning difficulties.

Research suggests that the problems of parents with learning difficulties living in the community are similar to those encountered by other parents of the same socio-economic status (Unger and Howes 1986). Their parenting styles also do not seem to differ from those of other parents in similar circumstances (Andron and Tymchuk 1987). As Brantlinger (1988) warns, it is 'important to distinguish the effects of social class from the effects of mental retardation on parenting skills'. After allowing for the effects of previous institutionalized living (Dowdney et al. 1985), much of the inadequate child care among parents with learning difficulties may be seen as the product of poverty (Fotheringham 1980; 1981). As Schilling et al. (1982) have observed, 'mentally retarded parents are relegated to socio-economic circumstances that foster child maltreatment'. Consequently, it is not surprising to find that parents with learning difficulties who come to the attention of child protection services share many characteristics with parents in the general population who experience similar caretaking problems (Rosenberg and McTate 1982). Foremost among these are inadequate incomes, unemployment, poor vocational skills, a disadvantaged childhood, isolation from their extended family, an insufficiency of social supports, stressed marital relationships, and a lack of ordinary life experiences (Mickelson 1949). In short, the factors that make it hard for parents with learning difficulties to cope are mostly the same as those that make it hard for people who do not have learning difficulties to be good parents (Gath 1988).

A number of good practice principles emerge from these points. Practitioners must:

- avoid blaming the victim by ascribing poor childrearing to the limitations of the parents where it owes more to the constraints of their social situation;
- be sensitive to the similarities between the parenting problems of people with learning difficulties and those of other at-risk families, and respond in a like-minded way;
- beware of underestimating the contribution which practical supports can make to helping families under pressure.

Research point 4: The problems of many parents stem more from their own upbringing than from their learning difficulties.

Parents with learning difficulties are 'very unlikely to have had experiences in childhood that offered any model of good-enough parenting' (Gath 1988). Many, especially among the current generation of parents, will have spent some or all of their childhood and adolescence in institutions of one kind or another. Others will have experienced poor parenting themselves or have led a sheltered and protected family life. As Schilling et al. (1982) point out, people with learning difficulties tend to be disadvantaged in each of the three main ways that most people learn about childrearing: direct experience, observation and reading.

Institutional living does not prepare a person to be an adequate parent (Tymchuk 1990b). As Brandon (1957) has commented, 'if a girl gets any sort of training in an institution, it is usually in housework, not in child care or human relationships'. This fact underlines the dangers of generalizing about the parenting abilities of people with learning difficulties on the basis of evidence drawn primarily from those raised in institutions. Donaldson (1992), for instance, describes a support group for parents most of whom had spent their early lives in hospital. She found 'their knowledge of family life was poor, and their awareness of parenting skills was very low. Few of them had good parenting models on which to base their own behaviour.' These deficits and the problems to which they give rise are not unique to people with learning difficulties. Quinton et al. (1984) followed into adult life a cohort of girls brought up in children's homes and found that 'institutional rearing . . . significantly predisposed to poor parenting'. This finding is expanded by Dowdney et al. (1985) who report that the ex-care women in their study were 'not particularly skilful in picking up their children's cues or in responding to their children's needs'.

Aside from the absence of parenting models, one reason for these difficulties, as Andron and Tymchuk (1987) observe, is that parents with an institutional background 'have been socialized to be highly dependent'. They have had little opportunity to make their own decisions or to learn the independent coping skills that parenthood requires. Consequently, they are more likely to succumb when faced with chronic stress and disadvantage in adult life (Quinton et al. 1984). A supportive spouse can help to offset the detrimental effects of an institutional upbringing, but research suggests that women from such a background are more likely to marry men with problems (ibid.). One way or another, as Whitman et al. (1990) advise, working successfully with mothers means never underestimating 'the power and influence wielded by the man in their lives'.

For people who grow up in a home rather than in an institution, family living offers no guarantee of appropriate models of parenting. Many parents will themselves have experienced inadequate nurturing and sexual victimization by their own families. Turk and Brown (1992) describe the sexual abuse of people with learning difficulties as 'a significant and serious problem'. Almost one-third of the cases uncovered by their survey involved the abuse of people living at home with their families, and in just over a third of cases the perpetrator was either a family member or a friend/neighbour. In a study of families referred for child maltreatment, Seagull and Scheurer (1986) found that 'most low functioning parents (75%) came from chaotic and abusive backgrounds'. This finding is consistent with other research showing that, where a child had been admitted to care, the parenting difficulties were almost always associated with serious adversities in the childhood of one or both parents (Quinton and Rutter 1984a; 1984b).

However, even parents who have enjoyed a loving and secure upbringing in a stable family often enter 'parenthood without the benefit of training for adulthood' (Andron and Tymchuk 1987). Where families never expect them to become parents, possibly assigning them the role of perennial child, they may be denied even an elementary induction into the parental role – looking after brothers and sisters, babysitting, being left in charge of the house, participating in family decisions – such as forms part of most people's growing up.

The implications for practitioners are that they should:

- always ensure that people's parenting abilities and problems are assessed in the context of their own lives and experience;
- ensure that parents with learning difficulties are not treated more punitively than other parents whose problems similarly stem from a disadvantaged upbringing;
- be wary of underestimating the importance of the role played by fathers/partners;
- be prepared to show patience and understanding in helping people to address their early experience;
- be alert to the possibly damaging effects of physical, sexual or system abuse on parents' own functioning.

Research point 5: Parents with learning difficulties are more likely to experience parenting under conditions of adversity and are also more susceptible to these strains.

For most parents with learning difficulties family life is constantly under threat. Shortage of money, debt, unemployment, chronic housing problems, fraught relationships, the hardships of single parenthood. personal harassment, victimization and skill deficits all contribute to their vulnerability. As long as families are preoccupied by such crises of day-to-day survival their capacity for dealing with the demands of parenting and child development will be reduced (Espe-Sherwindt and Kerlin 1990). It is against these demands, however, that their 'fitness for parenthood' is judged. Consequently, overarching all other pressures, parents live with the ever-present fear that their children may be taken away (Andron and Tymchuk 1987). Usually under close surveillance from the statutory services, families feel their every move is under scrutiny and any mistake risks punitive consequences.

Within the psychology of learning, stress is generally presented as a form of overload on an individual's adaptive resources. Lazarus (1966), for example, suggests that environmental pressures are perceived as more stressful for people with fewer available resources and supports. Parkes (1971) also notes that those with poor coping skills are particularly vulnerable to the traumatic effects of stress: decreased functioning, depression, withdrawal, anger and fear. In this light, parents with learning difficulties appear to face a sort of double jeopardy. More likely to experience parenting under conditions of adversity, they are also more susceptible to its strains. If so then, as Feldman (1986) has commented, given the range and variety of pressures these parents encounter, their adaptability and durability is often extraordinary.

The general lessons for practitioners are that they should:

- explore practical ways of reducing the pressures on the family from environmental threats, so lightening the parental load;
- be ready to respond to early signs of stress instead of waiting for a crisis to occur;
- ensure that parents have access to independent, informed and sympathetic advice whenever issues relating to parental responsibilities and the care of the children arise.

Research point 6: The parenting skills of people with learning difficulties can be improved by training.

The research evidence shows that, like other parents, mothers and fathers with learning difficulties have the potential to develop new skills and their parenting abilities can be improved by training (Thompson 1984; Budd and Greenspan 1985; Feldman et al. 1985; 1986; 1989; Tymchuk et al. 1988; Whitman and Accardo 1990; Whitman et al. 1989; Tymchuk and Feldman 1991). In a summary of this work, Tymchuk et al. (1990) conclude that the interactions between mothers and their children 'can become more positive and less punitive through some form of systematic intervention'. The lessons from this research are examined more closely in the next section.

Practitioners should always allow for the possibility of personal growth and new learning by:

- never assuming that parenting deficits are irremediable;
- never underestimating people's capacity to change;
- accepting responsibility for ensuring that parents are given the opportunity to acquire adequate child care skills and to learn appropriate parenting behaviour;
- never seeking permanently to remove a child from home for reasons of neglect, inadequate care or abuse by omission before every effort has been made to equip the parents with the skills they need to cope.

Research point 7: Adequate social supports are a significant factor in protecting against parenting breakdown.

Just as adequate parenting is not a simple function of intelligence neither is there a simple relationship between parental competence and child outcome (Tucker and Johnson 1989). One reason is that the support system may compensate for shortcomings in the skills of the parents to ensure satisfactory care for the children. Indeed, a significant predictor of child well-being is the adequacy of supports that parents have 'regardless of their own level of knowledge and skill' (Tymchuk 1992).

Working with parents with learning difficulties is a challenge for professionals. Often the framework of supportive services is lacking (Crain and Millor 1978). Public prejudice and discrimination serve to deter or exclude people from using mainstream services such as family planning clinics, ante-natal classes, adult education, voluntary groups for single parents and so on (Madsen 1979). The inability to read or write may further reinforce their isolation by limiting access to services and to information about their rights and entitlements. Moreover, many parents have had such bad experiences of the services that their main aim becomes one of avoiding them in the future so further cutting themselves off from potential sources of support or help in a crisis (Whitman et al. 1989). Together these factors often push families into overtaxing their informal support network (Rosenberg and McTate 1982), a consideration which may also help to explain why they appear to get so little physical support from their own extended families (Andron and Tymchuk 1987). The corollary of such a breakdown (or the absence of informal caretakers) may be an overload of the case management system (Whitman et al. 1990). Indeed, there may be a level at which it becomes impractical to deliver the support necessary to enable parents to go on looking after their children but 'the existence and location of that cutoff point needs to be proven on a case-by-case basis, and not presumed' (Whitman et al. 1989).

Responsible professional involvement in the families of parents with learning difficulties calls for (Miller 1981; Espe-Sherwindt and Kerlin 1990):

- a long-term view, a long-term commitment and a genuine appreciation of the parents as people;
- an enabling approach aimed at creating opportunities for parents to develop and exhibit their competence;
- a user-centred framework that gives parents a sense of control over their own and their children's lives.

Research on training

In recent years, evidence about the effectiveness and limits of parenting training has been growing as a result of the pioneering efforts of practitioners and researchers, primarily in North America. A bibliography of published training programme curricula is provided in Tymchuk (1990b) – see also Craft (1993) and McGaw (1993). Overall, the findings are positive (Tymchuk and Feldman 1991) although they need to be appraised in context.

Most of the reported work in this field has focused on training in personal and interactive skills (such as how to talk to the child, how to play with the child, the use of reinforcers, methods of discipline) rather than on practical ones (like timekeeping, household management, health and hygiene, home safety). This is because the underlying concern has been with the prevention of developmental delay or cultural retardation in the child rather than the support of the family for its own sake. The training needs of parents have mainly been determined by practitioners with the parents' own perspective generally being overlooked (Llewellyn 1991; Walton-Allen and Feldman 1991). Programmes have tended to use the techniques of behaviour modification and to concentrate on training in the clinic rather than in the home. Moreover, training has been directed almost exclusively to mothers and virtually no information is available about its impact on family functioning. Lastly, the target groups have been skewed towards the more able people and there is a need for further research into the receptivity of parents at various levels of ability.

Although there is no reason to doubt that parents can be taught to acquire new parenting skills, there are three main areas of uncertainty in the literature about the effectiveness of training. The first concerns whether the skills acquired are maintained over time after training is discontinued. Rapid learning may be followed by quick forgetting without ongoing reinforcement. Peterson et al. (1983), for example, found that positive benefits disappeared quickly whereas Feldman et al. (1989) report that most (but not all) newly acquired skills were sustained over a follow-up period of between three and 18 months. It is not possible to tell whether these different outcomes were related to parental or programme differences. The second area of mixed evidence concerns whether people are able to generalize from their learning in the sense of transferring the lessons across settings (for example, from clinic to home) or applying them in new situations. Finally, there is a measure of uncertainty about whether parents can learn to adjust their parenting styles to fit the changing needs of a growing child.

Putting aside these qualifications, however, a number of empirically grounded points that serve as guidelines for policy and practice can be gleaned from the current research literature.

Training point 1: Training can improve the knowledge and skills of mothers in virtually all areas of parenting, although the extent of learning varies between individuals.

Training point 2: Periodic and ongoing long-term 'refresher' support is needed to maintain learned skills.

Training point 3: Success in training is related to prior parental competence – although competence itself does not bear any direct relationship to IQ which may be less important than interest in and involvement with the child and the parent's motivation to learn.

Training point 4: Training is less effective where parents are having to cope with external pressures in their lives (such as debt, homelessness, harassment, the protective agencies, opposition from their extended family) and are preoccupied with the crises of day-to-day survival.

Training point 5: The acquisition of new skills is more likely and training more effective where clearly specified, individualized goals are set and presented in small, discrete and concrete steps.

Training point 6: The maintenance and generalization of new learning is assisted by teaching in real-life settings rather than in the classroom or clinic, and by the involvement and support of fathers or partners.

Training point 7: Training must be geared to parental learning characteristics – for example, their slower rate of learning, inability to read, low self-esteem, difficulties in organizing, sequencing and sticking to time schedules, need for more intensive and continuous supervision – and a heavy initial investment in establishing trust and rapport will improve participation.

Training point 8: Training tends to be more effective when it is intensive, consistent and continuous rather than irregular, infrequent and provided by different agencies or changing staff.

Training point 9: Trainers themselves need to be experienced in working with people with learning difficulties.

Training point 10: A positive relationship between trainer and parent is one of the most valuable curriculum resources.

Research on support

Almost fifty years ago, Mickelson (1949), addressing the question of whether parents with learning difficulties could be helped to give their children better care, answered with a firm yes. 'Today's challenge', she declared, 'is to show how it can be done.' We have still to face up to this challenge. Adequate support services for parenting are almost non-existent. Yet the best predictor of neglect 'appears to be the absence of suitable societal or familial supports' (Tymchuk 1992).

The presence of a benefactor has been found to be crucial in enabling parents to continue looking after their children (Kaminer et al. 1981). The one feature that has consistently been shown to distinguish families where the children remained at home from families where the children were removed is the presence of another adult (or possibly several people) able to give support as required with matters beyond the parents' own coping resources (Andron and Sturm 1973; Floor et al. 1975: Seagull and Scheurer 1986; Espe-Sherwindt and Kerlin 1990). Edgerton (1967) defined a benefactor as someone without learning difficulties who helps with the practical difficulties of coping with everyday problems. The role may be filled by a relative, neighbour, employer, landlord, spouse or partner. Seagull and Scheurer (1986) typify the level of help needed by families as approximating 'that offered by a well-functioning extended family system'.

In contrast to the help given by benefactors, professional workers often impose considerable stress on families (McConachie 1991). The presumption of incompetence and their 'at-risk' status ensure that most parents are kept under close and constant supervision. Families often have many different workers involved at once, all taking up time, offering advice, encroaching on family life. Most are very aware of being watched, and of being judged against stringent standards. As Andron and Tymchuk (1987) observe, not many people are required to open up their homes to the type of scrutiny to which they are exposed. Perhaps inevitably it sometimes leads to resentment (Bass 1963–64), and a reluctance to seek or accept help that service providers interpret as an inability to use the health and social services (Johnson and Clark, 1984; Whitman and Accardo, 1990).

According to Zetlin et al. (1985), indigenous networks exhibit a number of advantages over formal services in the delivery of support to parents. They are local, familiar, reliable and the help given is non-stigmatizing, non-intrusive and based on standards rooted in the common cultural and class experience of members. These points lend further weight to the view that professional services may not always present a very good fit with parents' views of their own needs (Llewellyn, 1991; Walton-Allen and Feldman, 1991).

They are also consistent with the observation that the value of support to parents with learning difficulties is determined in large measure by the attitude of its providers (Tymchuk 1990b). Social support may be either 'competence-promoting' or 'competence-inhibiting' and the perception of parental competence directly affects the nature of the support provided (Tucker and Johnson 1989; see also Chapter 5). Benefactors and service providers must believe in the parents' ability and provide the opportunities for competence to emerge. Espe-Sherwindt and Kerlin (1990) found that families whose children were permanently removed typically had only limited support, lost their support at a crucial time or were viewed as incompetent by key figures within their support system. So far as professionals in particular are concerned, their values and attitudes towards parents with learning difficulties are likely to be just as important in providing effective support as their knowledge and skills. As Andron and Tymchuk (1987) have said, 'a professional must be really committed to working with these families and able to see their strengths as well as their problems'.

The research on supports for parenting, taken in the context of the wider literature on parents with learning difficulties, points to a number of good practice guidelines:

Support point 1: Respect for and support of the emotional bond between parent(s) and children should be the starting point for any intervention in the family.

Support point 2: Support should be provided to parents and children as people first.

Support point 3: Parents should be enabled to participate in the making of decisions which have a bearing on their family life or on the welfare of their children.

Support point 4: Support tends to be most effective when it is consistent, non-intrusive and non-threatening.

Support point 5: Support is more effective when directed to the survival and maintenance needs of families, followed by child care tasks, than to modifying styles of interaction within the family.

Support point 6: Service providers must be responsive to any informal support system already in place and ensure they do not interfere with its functioning.

Support point 7: Problems often arise when a family in difficulty is forced to turn for help to the very professionals with the main statutory responsibility for child protection.

Support point 8: The attitude of those who deliver the support is a crucial factor determining its effectiveness.

Support point 9: Services need to be organized in such a way that parents are made to feel competent, have a hand in solving their own problems and feel in control of events.

Support point 10:   A parent–child relationship based on love and affection is more easily supported than replaced.

Overview

The problems encountered by parents are rarely caused only by their learning difficulties (Lynch and Bakley 1989). Indeed, such parents share many characteristics with parents in the general population who have similar caretaking problems (Rosenberg and McTate 1982). Just as with any other group of parents, few safe generalizations can be made about the parenting abilities of mothers and fathers with learning difficulties (Budd and Greenspan 1984). A range of factors over and above a person's learning difficulties play a part in determining that person's adequacy as a parent and may make it hard to maintain good-enough standards of child care. The following obstacles to parenting are most widely cited in the literature:

- poverty, unemployment, limited vocational skills, inadequate housing, debt, lack of transportation;
- marital disharmony and family discord, family size and birth spacing, poor mental health in the spouse, isolation from extended family;
- childhood adversities and inadequate nurturing, institutional upbringing, lack of ordinary family experience and appropriate models of parenting behaviour;
- inadequate support services, lack of good legal representation, negative perceptions of parental competence within the service system, high visibility to child protection authorities;
- discrimination, stigma, prejudice, harassment and victimization, system abuse;
- real limitations in parenting skills, caretaking abilities and the capacity for household management.

These factors underscore the importance of locating an individual's functioning as a parent in its wider social context (Quinton et al. 1984). They also bear out Mickelson's (1949) observation that parents with learning difficulties are properly seen 'not as a different kind of parent but as a more vulnerable one'.

CHAPTER 3

Life stories and depth interviewing

Involving people with learning difficulties as informants in research is a fairly recent development. Less than ten years ago, Richards (1984) could identify only five British studies in the previous 20 years which had done so. This picture has now changed significantly. There has been increasing acknowledgment of the importance of listening to people with learning difficulties (Atkinson and Williams 1990). Numerous studies have been done in hospitals (Cattermole et al. 1987; Booth et al. 1990), in hostels (Brandon and Ridley 1983; Malin 1983; Sugg 1987), in Social Education Centres (Booth and Fielden 1992), in staffed houses and independent living schemes (Passfield 1983; Lowe et al. 1986; Flynn 1989) where people with learning difficulties have served as informants (see also Welsh Office-SSI,1991a; 1991b; 1991c). With a few notable exceptions, however (see, for example, Bogdan and Taylor 1982; Potts and Fido 1990), very little work has been done using the techniques of depth interviewing and the life story approach. Perhaps this is because, following Plummer (1983), researchers have too readily assumed that the subjects in this kind of study 'should be fairly articulate, able to verbalise and "have a good story to tell"'.

Yet the use of a biographical approach with people with learning difficulties would appear to have much in its favour. Where the task is to understand the subjective realm of the lived life, it is essential for the researcher first of all to listen to those who know. In the matter of their own lives, people with learning difficulties are 'expert witnesses' who speak from a secure position of knowledge. Life stories based on first person accounts provide 'an inner view of the person not accessible through other methods of data collection' (Birren and Deutchman 1991). At the same time, the biographical method gives access through the lives of individuals to structural features of their social world (Kohli 1981). This entails the researcher 'listening beyond' (Bertaux-Wiame 1981) the words of any particular informant to pick up the echoes of other people's experiences. Such common elements in their stories reveal how their lives are shaped by the wider society and throw light on the network of social relations to which they belong (Bertaux and Bertaux-Wiame 1981). In this way, as Ferrarotti (1981) has observed, the 'effort to understand a biography in all its uniqueness . . . becomes the effort to interpret a social system'.

In this chapter we explore some issues and problems in using the technique of depth interviewing with people who have learning difficulties. We aim to describe the methods used in researching this book, to provide some practical guidance in the use of biographical methods based on our own experience, and to argue for the utility of the life story approach with people who have learning difficulties. Contrary to Plummer's advice about the qualities of good informants, the people we interviewed often had poor speech and articulation skills, and some had limited recall. But their stories of joy and suffering are no less powerful for that, and none the less illuminating.

Managing the field relationship

Ethical considerations

Before starting the study we tried to clarify the broad ethical principles that would guide the investigation and mediate our relations with people in the field. We took our cue from the guiding principle of the self-advocacy movement: namely, that people with learning difficulties are people first (see, for example, People First of Washington 1985). This means they have the same value, rights (to choice, respect, dignity, self-determination and so on) and responsibilities as other adults. From this viewpoint, they should receive the same ethical treatment and consideration as any other subjects of research enquiry.

We recognized, however, that some people might present particular vulnerabilities that could not be overlooked. In such cases we chose to be guided by a fundamental tenet of the citizen advocacy movement which requires that the advocate (or, in our case, the researcher) treats the interests of their partner (here, the research subject) as if they were their own (O'Brien 1987). In other words, our obligation to the parents always came before the interests of the research whenever the two appeared to pull in different directions.

Obtaining consent

The nature of our research involved more than just eliciting people's co-operation in giving an interview. They were being invited to open the private world of their everyday lives to outside scrutiny. Asking people to participate in such a study when many would have been let down, maltreated and abused in the past by people they knew and trusted (including family and professionals) had to be undertaken with sensitivity and caution. It could not be done on the doorstep.

Our approach to obtaining consent was to establish contact on terms that left the initiative with the subject. Usually this entailed making an introduction through a professional worker who was already known and liked by the family. The worker was thoroughly briefed on the aims and methods of the study and it was then left up to him or her to explain the research to the parents and to ask if they would be willing to meet us. The workers decided when and how best to raise the matter with the families. In a few cases, for example, an approach was deferred for a number of weeks where the workers felt the time was not ripe because of a pending court case or because children had recently been removed from the care of their parents. Only after the parents had agreed to see us were we given their names and addresses. Once consent had been obtained, we also asked the worker involved if there were any particularly sensitive areas about which we would need to be cautious, especially with regard to the children, although we found such information was not always accurate.

This approach had a number of advantages: the research was introduced by someone known to the parents; it overcame the problem of confidentiality regarding the release of names by the statutory agencies; and it made refusal easier for the parent(s), so minimizing the risk of compliance often encountered among people with learning difficulties. It also helped to make the first interview less stressful as the parents had already indicated they wanted to see us and they, in turn, had some idea of what we wanted of them.

The disadvantages of this approach were that people's responses might be influenced by their relationship with the worker or by their perception of the agency; a lack of control over how the study was first presented and explained to people; and the risk that the researcher might come to be too closely identified with authority. Certainly, some workers' instincts were to refuse on behalf of the parents, and on one occasion we were told the parents had refused when we suspect they were not asked. Also, the care they put into explaining the study to parents undoubtedly varied such that not everyone had fully grasped what it was about when we met them. On balance, however, we are satisfied that the approach was both effective and ethically sound.

Establishing trust

Having made contact with the parents, the next step was to establish a trusting relationship. In the first instance, this meant being accepted as a person. While agreeing to see us, the parents' commitment at this stage had to be regarded as strictly conditional. They may have wanted to look us over and test us out before agreeing to proceed any further. Equally, they may have wanted confirmation of our good faith before revealing more about themselves.

Broadly speaking, there are two ways of looking at trust: as a form of mutually beneficial exchange, or as a form of moral currency. In the exchange model, trust is a function of reciprocity in the relationship between the researcher and the subject where each gives the other something they desire or need. As a moral status, on the other hand, trust is dependent on the actions and attitudes of the researcher which must both validate the researcher's identity and purpose as well as show that the subject is valued as a person in his or her own right. While a number of people in our study appreciated being able to talk to a sympathetic outsider (and some workers were keen to put us in touch with parents for precisely that reason), our approach was based more on a moral understanding of trusting relationships.

In the beginning it was necessary for the interviewer to make sure the parents understood the methods and purpose of the study, the confidential status of the research, and the reasons for using a tape recorder. It was also important to reassure them that their names would not be revealed in any published written work and that only their stories would be used. The interviewer emphasized at the outset that if, at any stage, the parents were unhappy about the interviews they should let their contact worker know and we would pull out without question.

The parents themselves were always left to decide where and when (if at all) the next meeting took place. Such appointments were used more to gauge whether they still wanted us to call than to plan our own workload. For most, time was marked by means other than a clock, diary or calendar – by when the mobile shop came, benefit days, television programmes. In the few cases where the parents had a telephone, we generally rang the day before an appointment to confirm our visit and remind them we were coming. Otherwise it was necessary to call round, hope they were at home, and ask if it was still convenient for us to talk.

Building rapport

Our aim was to understand people's experience as parents in terms sympathetic to the meaning and significance they gave to events in their lives and faithful to their interpretation of them. This would not be achieved by a 'hit and run' approach. Building rapport demands a measure of intimacy that goes beyond the normal relationship between interviewer and informant. Although there is no easy recipe for success, we were guided by a few simple precepts. First, we treated rapport as a two-way process of communication involving both information gathering and giving. We were happy to answer personal questions, to give people our home address and telephone number, and to let them know we would be pleased to hear from them if ever they wanted to contact us (and many did). As Ferrarotti (1981) has observed, the price paid by the researcher for an intimate and personal knowledge of an informant is 'to be reciprocally known just as thoroughly by the latter'. Second, we consciously tried to set aside the values and standards of middle class society – in judging such things as homemaking skills, childrearing practices, the quality of family life or parental competence – and endeavoured instead to take people as we found them. Third, we followed a rule of trying to be absolutely straight with people and always delivering when we said we would do something (such as being punctual, keeping appointments, returning phone calls, obtaining information and so on).

As others, too, have found (Wyngaarden 1981), many informants saw the researcher as a possible helper with their problems, as someone who might be able to obtain necessary services or speak up for them with professionals. Our response was generally to remind them of our role as researchers and to avoid being seen as potential benefactors. Occasionally, however, we found ourselves in a situation where help was not only needed but needed immediately. To maintain a detached stance at these times was neither possible in human terms nor desirable on research grounds.

There are dangers for researchers in building up close personal ties with the people they are studying. Indeed, these dangers give rise to some of the most common criticisms of biographical methods, including charges of lack of objectivity, implicit or a priori conceptualization and arbitrariness (Allport 1947; Gaston 1982). Such ties, the argument runs, engender feelings of friendship, loyalty and affection which may cloud the researcher's judgement, bias his or her perceptions and otherwise compromise the capacity for critical detachment on which objectivity depends. While accepting the force of these points, we hold to the position adopted by Birren and Deutchman (1991) that methods of data analysis are available for managing such problems (see, for example, Glaser and Strauss 1967; Denzin 1970; Thompson 1981). We accord greater weight to the importance for our research of developing personal relationships of trust and rapport. Both these qualities may have a fundamental bearing on the validity of people's subjective accounts of their own experience. Informants may have many things they would ordinarily choose to hide from a stranger and a myriad reasons for garnishing the truth. Rather than being an indulgence, trust and rapport may have a crucial influence on the quality of the data obtained.

Withdrawing

Having built up close personal relationships with the parents, based on frequent contact over an extended period of time, the task of withdrawing when the research finished had to be approached with care and sensitivity. People with learning difficulties usually have a restricted social network comprising mainly members of their immediate family, paid or voluntary workers or other people with learning difficulties (Richardson and Ritchie 1989). Relationships such as ours might assume a greater importance in their lives than we can readily imagine. We felt it would be unethical to pull out abruptly just because the process of data gathering had been completed. Accordingly, we determined to withdraw from each family at their own pace and only when they were ready. In most cases this was negotiated mutually and quite smoothly. Some relationships, however, have extended well beyond the research. Social researchers using biographical methods must be prepared to live up to this commitment or risk their field relationships becoming exploitative.

Managing the interviews

The first meeting

Our initial plan was to use the first meeting for introductions rather than for data gathering. We saw this session mainly as an opportunity for breaking the ice, beginning to get to know each other, and allaying any anxieties people might have about our motives. We also wanted to ensure that parents understood what we were doing and why, and what was being asked of them. The only information they had about the project at this point was what they had been given by the professional worker who originally acted as go-between. In order to ensure that everyone was properly briefed we felt it was important to clarify these matters and to allow them another chance of pulling out. For all these reasons we had not intended to record or document these first meetings.

In the event, things did not work out quite so neatly. Some people launched straight into their story almost after the first hello without any encouragement or prompting. In such cases, where the person was obviously eager and willing to talk, we simply waited for the first natural break to ask their permission to record and began the interview immediately. Others were obviously emotionally stressed and wanting to unburden their feelings to a sympathetic listener. This was especially true of parents whose children had recently been taken from them. In these cases, they were given the space and support to say what they had to say; no attempt was made to record or make notes (although a process record was written up afterwards); and the interviewer acted merely as a listening-post without trying to direct the informant's flow.

Careful attention to how we presented ourselves was an important part of establishing trust and building rapport. All the parents in our study had experienced repeated and often painful dealings with health and social workers whom most regarded with suspicion if not outright hostility. It was essential for us to avoid being tarred with the same brush and quickly to dissociate ourselves from 'the welfare'. (On one occasion a formidable, matriarchal grandmother and her four sons sat in on the first meeting with her daughter and son-in-law to vet the interviewer and police the interview.) This was not easy as our accents, way of speaking, manners and dress (as well as the cars we drive) tended to bracket us with such professional types. Middle class people rarely visit their estates, never mind their homes, except on official business. We found the most effective answer was to be truthful. We said we were writing a book on families like them who had some sort of involvement with community nurses or social workers; that we were interested in what they thought about the help and support they had received; and that, while our work might not benefit them personally, we hoped it would do some good for other families in a similar situation. People were genuinely engaged by the idea that others might benefit from their experience. Perhaps, too, some were flattered by the prospect of featuring in a book.

On the basis of our experience with the first few parents, we quickly developed a set of flexible ground rules for handling the first meeting:

- Take your cue from the informant and be prepared to adapt according to their emotional needs and responses.
- Generally speaking, just listening is the best approach.
- Do not go in with a predetermined set of questions to ask or topics to discuss.
- Allow the informant to dictate what and how much is talked about.
- Do not feel pressured to record; you can always return to points again later.
- Any data collected at the first meeting should be regarded as a bonus.

Using the tape recorder

Consent was always sought on each and every occasion a recorder was used. At the first interview, a full explanation was given of why we wanted to record what was said, what use would be made of the material, and who would have access to the tapes. All informants were guaranteed confidentiality. At subsequent interviews, people were asked more casually: the interviewer would say something like 'Do you mind?' as the machine was brought out. A few did withhold their permission, suggesting that people did not agree merely out of deference.

Tape recording is a vital aid when verbatim narratives are required but there are times in compiling life stories when other means of data collection might be more appropriate or when recording is neither desirable nor possible. An interview should not be regarded as wasted if it cannot be recorded. It is always important to let the situation and the purpose of the interview determine whether or not a recorder is used rather than allow the recorder to determine the purpose or conduct of the interview.

For recording imposes its own constraints. It can inhibit people from speaking their minds even when they raise no objections to being recorded. A telltale sign of this effect was the number of people who said something like, 'Ooh, I was going to swear then and you've got that thing on'. Clearly they were conscious of it even if the interviewer was not. Another was the tendency for people to disclose sensitive and confidential information only after the recorder had been switched off. At first we blamed ourselves for having terminated the interview too abruptly, before realizing that people were choosing to hold some things back until they felt it was safer to voice them.

Recording can be a stressful business where the interviewer does not have control over the interview situation, and a potentially risky or costly one where the quality of recording cannot be assured. Thus, for example, trying to record in busy or noisy environments – with the TV or radio on, a washing machine working, a baby fretting, children playing, a budgie chirruping or someone using power tools in the next room – can upset the interviewer's concentration. Background interference of this sort is mostly intrusive only if you are wanting to record. When the aim is to establish a non-threatening relationship in which the informant feels safe enough to talk openly it sometimes may not be advisable to emphasize one's role as a researcher by asking for quiet. Doing so might also make for a more formal and less relaxed interview. Good depth interviewing means allowing the informant to feel in control. With this in mind, it is especially important on people's home ground for the interviewer to fit into rather than try to stage manage the situation. It is crucial not to let the demands of recording override such considerations.

Problems of sound quality also arise for other reasons. People with speech problems, strong accents, poor pronunciation and articulation, or quiet voices, as well as interviews involving several people where there is a lot of cross-talk or simultaneous chatter, can all make for transcription difficulties (and add to transcription costs). In such cases it may be easier and more effective to make notes instead of using a recorder. Certainly it is important to have tapes transcribed immediately so that transcripts can be corrected, omissions made good and errors spotted while the interview is still fresh in the memory.

Researchers should not be afraid of putting the tape recorder aside (occasionally by choice, not just necessity). They can and should train themselves to reconstruct interviews afterwards. This calls for method and self-discipline. Immediately the interview is over, around the corner in the car, rough notes should be made of the main points or areas covered in the discussion, and any new information or particularly memorable quotes jotted down. At this stage it is better to record the outline rather than the detail of the interview. The ordering of the material is irrelevant: the secret is to get it down. Back home these notes should be filled out and put into order. Using them as prompts, and concentrating on a part of the interview at a time, as much detail as possible should be recorded. Visual images – where people were sitting, what they were doing, their facial expressions and similar behavioural cues – can all help to jog the memory and to bring back their words. After a long day the task can be exhausting, but with practice it is possible to reproduce faithful accounts of interviews that yield little in the way of utility to a recording.

Making notes during the interview obviates many of the advantages of not recording. It comes between the interviewer and the informant; it is just as intrusive as recording; and it diverts attention from the transactional side of the interview process. Notetaking might possibly be useful when detailed factual information is being collected (for example, on family history and relationships, dates of events and so on) and an informant has refused permission to use a recorder. In such instances, the informant's consent should always be obtained for making notes just as for tape recording.

Edgerton et al. (1984) acknowledge that tape recording may not be appropriate on some occasions. Recording puts the emphasis in data collection on the spoken word. By not using a recorder, other sources of data are opened up and ways of obtaining information other than by question and answer are made possible. For example, we accompanied parents on shopping trips, attended case reviews, visited people in hospital, dropped in at their day centre, went out for lunch together, attended birthday parties, went with them to court, to a family centre, to a women's group and so on. Such contacts enabled us to observe how the parents cope in different situations, how other people respond to them, how they work together as a couple, and to learn more about the quality of their relationships and the pattern of their lives. These shared experiences also allowed them to get to know us better and gave us much more to talk about – out of which has come new insight and understanding. Similarly, we sometimes chose deliberately not to record an interview in order to be free of the machine: free to move from room to room or out into the garden;

free to play with the children; free from having to think about the tape running out or the batteries going flat (we gave up using rechargeable batteries because of their trick of suddenly failing without warning); free from the subliminal pressure it exerts to keep the conversation going or bring the informant back to the point.

Sometimes the situation we encountered on a visit was clearly not made for recording. For example, one mother was found to be very depressed when we called and it seemed right to respond to her need to talk rather than to press ahead with an interview. Or again, for instance, we walked into homes where there was a tension in the air, like the after-shock of a marital quarrel, and people were obviously not ready to talk. The following extract from our research notes illustrates the kind of situation in which recording was not possible although the visit itself was worthwhile:

'10.15 am and another hot, dry day. The door of the caravan was shut and I hesitated to knock. Molly opened it in her dressing gown and invited me into the darkened interior. The two children were sitting having toast and jam for breakfast in their nightclothes and Kevin was dressed. Radio One was playing quietly. As soon as I entered Amy noticed that my shoes were like hers and she showed me. Kevin asked if I would like a cup of tea and I sat down. It was an interesting three-quarters of an hour watching the family prepare for the day. They seemed undisturbed by my presence and would throw me a piece of information now and then but there were easy silences. The children made a lot of fuss and brought me all sorts to look at. Tony had decided I was OK and sat on my knee and gave me a hug. Kevin helped dress them both while Molly dressed in the bedroom. Both children had been to the hairdressers and they looked most attractive. Amy brought her dress to show me, and Molly wanted me to look at the track suit she had bought Tony. I had a feeling that some effort was being made for my benefit but nevertheless it went very smoothly – washing, shaving, cleaning teeth (for my inspection), dressing, combing hair. I was even shown the cereals they have – sugar puffs and cocoa pops (cheaper brands).'

Finally, although our machine is not obtrusive (we favour a compact cassette recorder with built-in flat microphone) it does show we are there in a professional capacity, doing a job, and such a badge is not always helpful. Interestingly, from a personal point of view, we found it became harder to use the tape recorder as our relationships with parents developed.

Two general points about the use of tape recorders in depth interviewing are worth emphasising:

- Think carefully on each occasion and decide whether recording is necessary and desirable. Do not record merely as a matter of routine. Sometimes it might be better not to record.
- There is a strong case for deliberately not recording some sessions and using the opportunity so created to explore other ways of collecting data.

The follow-up interviews

Interviews were conducted as informal, open-ended conversations taken at the pace of the parents. Only one interviewer was ever involved with a family. In order to put people at their ease the interviewer never carried a briefcase or clipboard. The tape recorder was small enough to be kept in a pocket or handbag and, when in use, was placed discreetly out of view (usually on the floor).

Although commonly described as 'unstructured interviewing', this really is a misnomer. As Tremblay (1957) has pointed out, such interviews do have a structure 'in the sense that the interviewer, familiar with the type of material sought from the informant, has a framework of questions in mind'. We had prepared a nine-page *aide-mémoire* of topics to be explored with parents covering such things as their own childhood, their family history, their marriage/partnership, pregnancy, labour and confinement, babycare, childrearing, social supports, relationships, personal and/or family crises, and being a mother/father. Like a map to the rambler, however, it provided occasional bearings rather than a step-by-step guide. We used it as a checklist before and after each interview to mark off the areas that had been covered and to remind ourselves of those that remained to be addressed.

At the first interview proper, we would provide an introduction to the kind of topics we were interested in and leave it up to informants where they wished to start, encouraging them to develop the themes in their own way. In most cases there was no rush to cover the material. We were prepared to go back as many times as necessary until we knew what we wanted to know or felt there was little else we were likely to learn. The lack of pressure on time was a key factor in maintaining a conversational style of approach and allowing a dialogue to develop. It meant that the interviewer could take her cue from the informant; allow the conversation to take its natural course; pursue issues as they arose; postpone sensitive matters until trust was established; and follow digressions to see where they might lead. The characteristic feature of the life-story method is just such a dialogue based on a combination of exploration and questioning within a framework 'determined not by the researcher, but by the informant's view of his or her own life' (Thompson 1981).

We found it was important to begin the interviews without any fixed assumptions about people's ability to understand what was being asked of them. Their abilities had to be tested. Our approach was simply to talk as we would do normally, adapting our style – for instance, using simpler language, avoiding abstract questions, keeping to one point at a time – only if problems emerged. In this sense our technique was what Tremblay (1957) has described as 'self-developing' in that 'the researcher can refine [the] interviewing method during the course of a session, or through repeated contacts, as the amount of knowledge about the problem increases and as the ability of the informant is fully revealed'. One useful ploy for opening up or carrying forward a dialogue with informants was to ask to see their family photographs. Time and again this proved to be an excellent way of exploring family structure, family history and relationships as well as of putting informants at their ease.

Before each interview the transcript of the previous one (and possibly more if some time had elapsed since the last meeting) was read, carefully annotated and checked against the *aide-mémoire*. This preparation was vital in order to make the most of the interview, and out of politeness to the parents. In the early days it was a way of keeping up with who's who in each family, of learning the names and relationships of people in their social network, and of keeping track of their story to date – all of which was necessary in order to ask illuminating questions and to follow or pick up the nuances of what was being said. Later on, as the number of families in the study increased, their circumstances changed, and their stories grew more detailed, it was an essential means of reminding ourselves where we had got to with them. At every stage, a close rereading of the transcript enabled us to pick up cues we had overlooked during the course of the interview, hear things we had missed at the time, spot probes we had failed to make, see contradictions that called for clarification, pinpoint matters important to the parent(s) (as revealed, for example, by reiteration or force of language), identify issues that needed following up, or think of new questions to ask next time. Thoroughly steeped in what had gone before, we were then ready for the next interview.

Finally, it was important to know when to end an interview and leave. Once again this meant being attuned to the cues provided by the respondent. One such signal we found was the natural break in a conversation which appeared when the interviewer started asking questions that did not follow on from what the informant had been saying. At this point, the dialogue began to shade into something more like an interrogation. Sometimes, too, the researcher had to call a halt when concentration began to flag or when people started repeating themselves a lot.

Informants with learning difficulties

There is now an extensive literature on possible problems affecting the quality of data gathered using personal documents or biographical methods (see, for example, Allport 1947; Phillips 1971; Douglas 1976; Gittins 1979). It is not part of our purpose to go over this same ground. Instead we shall focus on issues of method linked to the fact that the majority of our informants were people who have learning difficulties.

Reliability and validity

Reliability and validity are notoriously slippery concepts in life story research. Even their relevance may be challenged. The approach is generally too time-consuming and intrusive to allow for replication, and the complexities of field relationships do not allow for standardization or control. Equally, lacking independent access to informants' inner world of experience, there is no easy way of validating their accounts and perceptions. Consequently, we have no sure way of knowing whether people with learning difficulties are any more or less problematical as informants than other subjects.

Three types of consistency check were possible on our data: across separate interviews involving the same informant; with other data sources (generally other family members or relatives, but occasionally official records); and with other families in a similar situation. All three checks present their own limitations.

Inconsistency between interviews is not necessarily a sign of bias. As trust developed over time people modified their accounts to reveal more about themselves. For example, one incest victim, who initially said the baby she had had by her father had been aborted, only revealed at the sixth interview that her son had in fact been adopted after she had looked after him for a while, and that he had recently sent her a card following his eighteenth birthday.

Other data sources might help to verify basic factual information (like age at first pregnancy, where a couple had met or how long they had known each other before they set up home together) but could not help to validate feelings or perceptions.

Making comparisons between families was perhaps the best technique for validating the experiential data: as one account confirms another, stories accrete and regularities emerge so it becomes less likely that individual narratives are the product of one person's fancy and more likely that they show structural features in the lives of the subjects. For instance, the most consistent feature of our parents' dealings with the support services was the inconsistent treatment they received.

Over and above these technical checks on the data, however, there remains the feeling human observer. Ultimately, in this type of research, the validity of the data is the stuff of the relationship between the interviewer and the informant. Someone who phones to ask when the researcher is going to call in again is unlikely to be an evasive respondent. Someone who reveals painful secrets from the past, gets angry or weeps real tears is not presenting a front or fooling themselves. It is through close personal contact that researchers slowly learn whether to believe what they are told. The first requirement here is time spent with the informant. This suggests that the problems of reliability and validity are more pronounced the greater the distance between researchers and their subjects.

Articulateness

Bertaux (1981) says that 'a good life story is one in which the interviewee *takes over the control of the interview situation* and talks freely' (emphasis in original). This rarely happened in our study and, except on a few occasions at the first interview, it was usually the partner without learning difficulties who took the lead in this way. Generally speaking, our informants were more inclined to answer questions with a single word, a short phrase or the odd sentence. The following extract from an interview is not untypical:

Int: When you were in the children's home, was your sister with you? Were you in together?
Resp: Yes.
Int: You won't remember your parents then?
Resp: No.
Int: And there's just the two of you, just you and your sister?
Resp: No, there's quite a few.
Int: Is she the one you're closest to then?
Resp: Yes. I've got another sister lives in Wakefield and I've got two brothers and a sister who live in Leeds as well.

Although our informants varied in their language skills, their conversation tended to display some or all of the following characteristics: an instrumental rather than an expressive vocabulary; a present orientation; a concrete rather than an abstract frame of reference; a literal rather than a figurative mode of expression; a focus on people and things rather than on feelings and emotions; and a responsive rather than a proactive style. None of these characteristics, of course, are unique to people with learning difficulties although the challenge presented to the researcher is perhaps more overt in their case. Most importantly, this lack of verbal fluency was not a barrier to the parents' telling their story. It does, however, have implications for the role of the interviewer (who must expect to have to work harder), the conduct of the interviews (techniques other than just talking have to be used to engage the informant), the length of time it takes to compile a life story (the full story emerges only slowly, a bit at a time), and the way it is written up.

Response bias

In a series of papers Sigelman and her colleagues have tested the proposition that due to 'deficient cognitive, verbal, and social skills, mentally retarded persons might be especially susceptible to response effects' (Sigelman et al. 1981a – see also, Sigelman et al. 1981b; 1982). They set out to investigate the impact of three such sources of bias: *responsiveness*, or the ability to answer the question; *acquiescence*, or the tendency to respond affirmatively regardless of the question; and *recency*, or the tendency to select the last option in either/or and multiple-choice questions.

Few of their respondents could answer open-ended questions adequately and those who could provided relatively little information. The use of examples or probes failed to increase responsiveness and created its own validity problems. On the other hand, simple yes/no questions significantly enhanced responsiveness but introduced a strong acquiescence bias. Either/or questions with discrete rather than quantitative options produced high responsiveness, good consistency and only a weak tendency for recency, although their utility on less than strictly factual topics remains to be established. Overall, Sigelman concludes that, despite the bias towards under-reporting, open-ended questions should be preferred to the yes/no variant on the grounds of response validity.

Sigelman's finding of under-reporting in response to open-ended questions matches our own experience of the lack of verbal fluency among our informants, but otherwise we have some doubts about the application of these findings to our study. Her research was done with samples of institutionalized children. For these groups, acquiescence may be an adaptive response to the demands of living when the greater part of their lives is under someone else's control. By contrast, the parents in our study have experienced a fuller life (including marriage, childbirth, bringing up a family, having their children taken away, managing a household and so on), and a greater load of responsibility and risk-taking. For them acquiescence is not a strategy for survival. This difference is well illustrated by one mother who left her family home and voluntarily admitted herself to a hostel for people with learning difficulties. Her public acquiescence with staff decisions was contradicted in private when she would vehemently express her dissent to the interviewer. When asked why she did not let them know how she felt, she reasoned that disagreeing with staff was one further problem she could do without. There is a danger, which Sigelman and her colleagues court, of regarding acquiescence as a function of people's disability rather than of their living situation.

Time and frequency

Flynn (1986) advises that questions about time and frequency are best avoided when interviewing people with learning difficulties – see also Atkinson (1988). This option was not open to us, given the aims of our research. A life story is essentially a narrative in time. We needed to know how long partners had been together, when people discovered they were pregnant, how often they saw their social worker or community nurse and so on. Where only one parent in a couple had learning difficulties the other was often on hand to provide this information. Where there was only a single parent or both had learning difficulties other ways around the problem had to be found. Four expedients in particular proved useful:

• Accuracy or exactness over dates and times was not always necessary and a rough approximation would suffice. For instance, people would often be able to distinguish between weeks and years and so be able to provide an idea of, say, the length of a relationship.
• Finding another marker was a helpful device. For instance, people were often able to say whether one thing had happened before or after another whose date was known; women could explain how long it was before they found they were pregnant by their size.
• Using the child(ren) as a chronometer. Although many parents had difficulty remembering their own age most knew the ages and birthdays of their children. Past events could be logged and dated in terms of how old their children were at the time.
• Knowing your informants and their habits of speech. For instance, one woman referred to a holiday arranged for the family by social services 'last year'. Knowing this to be a way of saying 'some years ago', the holiday was eventually dated by finding out that her eight year old son had been two at the time.

Joint interviews

A number of interviews involved a parent with learning difficulties and one or more other people – a partner, a close family member, an adult child, a support worker – without learning difficulties. These interviews presented a particular challenge and their own drawbacks and opportunities.

Often the person without learning difficulties threatened to dominate the conversation and the interviewer sometimes found it difficult not to collude by directing questions to the more articulate party or allowing that person to hold centre stage. Even questions addressed to the person with learning difficulties might be fielded by the other speaker. Also there was a danger of using language and modes of expression that unwittingly shut out the person with learning difficulties and prevented his or her participation. On one or two occasions we noticed that a person would interject with unrelated pieces of information in an attempt to draw themselves into the conversation. In collecting life stories, fluency itself can be a source of bias when it lures the interviewer away from the subject.

Joint interviews brought benefits, too. People with a common background and shared experience sparked off each other; mutual prompting encouraged the disclosure of things that might otherwise have been overlooked; often there was a degree of cross-questioning and challenging that an interviewer would not have entertained. Joint interviews involving relatives provided a fuller picture of the family as a unit. Also, informants who lacked confidence or were a little reticent were put at their ease by having a familiar face present.

We came to the view that joint interviews are useful for opening up new avenues of enquiry and tried to include them as part of our interviewing strategy. As a one-off or occasional device in a series of interviews their disadvantages were easily contained. Their drawbacks only became manifest when it was hard to get informants on their own: for example, because a support worker was always present in the home, because of the protective behaviour of a member of the extended family, or because one partner dominated. In such cases, special efforts had to be made to find space for people to tell their story, like taking them out somewhere or visiting them at their day centre or fixing a visit when it was known they would be alone.

Sensitive issues

Thompson (1981) comments that when a dialogue is established with an informant using the life story method 'the researcher comes to learn the unexpected as well as the expected'. Our experience supports this point. We have listened to alarming tales of rape, incest, child abuse, attempted suicide and rejection, and sat with bewildered and distraught parents as they relived the loss of their children or the hurt of their forced adoption.

Such disclosures place a lot of stress on an interviewer. There is the strain of witnessing and sharing the anguish of the informant, and the strain of coping with the feelings they release in oneself. There is also the worry of unleashing emotions that one may not know how to deal with or that might cause further pain to the informant. In order to help interviewers to handle these pressures it is important for them to have someone, bound by the rules of confidentiality that apply to the project as a whole, to whom they can unburden and who can provide emotional support.

There is also the strain arising from ethical dilemmas which such disclosures can create for the interviewer, especially when the principle of confidentiality comes into conflict with wider moral and legal responsibilities. Our position is that confidentiality must be upheld although interviewers should not be expected to carry the moral burden of their knowledge alone. To this end, we set up a reference group whose membership included a priest (cum advocate), an experienced researcher in the learning difficulties field, two co-workers from an advocacy group (one of whom has learning difficulties), and a senior social worker specializing in work with people who have learning difficulties. As well as providing independent monitoring of the study as a whole, one function of the reference group was to enable the researchers to share ethically sensitive or traumatic information (presented anonymously) in order to ease the load.

Concluding remarks

There is still a lot to learn about depth interviewing with people who have learning difficulties. Our study shows that it is a viable method which can produce new knowledge, new insights and a new perspective on their lives. In this chapter, we have set out some of the problems and challenges it presents, and outlined some of the techniques we found useful when following this approach. Hopefully others will be persuaded to build on and improve our work.

One final point calls for emphasis. The approach to depth interviewing described in this chapter is not so very different to the accounts in standard methodology texts or the techniques used in depth research with other devalued groups. There is a good reason for this fact. Parents with learning difficulties do not form a homogeneous group with a common history of family pathology. Their experiences of childrearing and parenting show more similarities than differences with other ordinary families from the same social background, and the problems they encounter or present tend to mirror those of other 'at risk' groups. As the process of normalization begins to influence the thinking of researchers as well as of practitioners in the learning difficulties field, it will perhaps become easier to accept that methods (such as depth interviewing) based on these similarities have a place in their work.

CHAPTER 4

Fitness for parenthood

Parents with learning difficulties are widely presumed to present a high risk of parenting breakdown. Successive studies have reported high rates for the removal of children from the family home (Mickelson 1949; Scally 1973; Accardo and Whitman 1990) and such evidence is often used to support a claim of parental inadequacy. Fotheringham (1980), for example, concludes that few parents have the ability to provide 'conditions of care at the minimal acceptable level'. Indeed, the rate of child removal is enough for Accardo and Whitman (1990) to assert that the only important question 'with regard to parenting failure of significantly mentally retarded adults would seem to be not whether but when'.

This chapter challenges this position by using the personal stories of parents to show that three variables commonly taken as indicating parental inadequacy – child care problems within the family; the admission of a child into care; and the termination of parental rights – cannot be taken at face value as evidence of lack of competence or parenting failure. Such outcomes are often mistakenly attributed to parenting deficits when they are more accurately viewed as deficiencies in professional practice, services or supports.

Parental competence and child outcomes

Of the 20 families involved in our study, 14 have had one or more of their children placed in short-term or permanent care. All eight parents who themselves spent most of their childhood in residential homes or hostels have had at least one of their children adopted or fostered. Almost all the families (19) admitted to having experienced child care problems at some time. The only exception was a mother who lived with her own parents.

Nine families had children with behaviour problems serious enough to call for outside intervention or the removal of the child. At the time of the study, 14 of the 36 children for whom information was available (excluding some of those, for example, who had been adopted, fostered or who were living with another parent outside the study) had been ascertained as having learning difficulties.

On the surface, these facts appear to lend support to the idea that mothers and fathers with learning difficulties characteristically exhibit a range of skill deficits that make it difficult for them to function as competent parents. A closer examination of their personal stories, however, reveals a more complex picture that suggests any such unqualified interpretation may seriously misrepresent their experience. The following eight categories of cases are all represented among the study families, some of whom fall into more than one category.

1. Parents whose only child was taken away at birth or very soon after and placed for adoption or put into permanent care.

2. Parents whose first child was removed but who have successfully raised subsequent children.

These parents were not given an opportunity to demonstrate their capacity to look after the child either because of intervention by the statutory services or because of pressure from their families.

In the former case, parental rights were terminated on the basis of a presumption of incompetence founded on the misplaced belief that adequate parenting is a function of intelligence. The decision amounted to a prospective finding of parenting failure (Gilhool and Gran, 1985) owing more to the prejudices and stereotypes of professionals – including the view that people are incapable of new learning – than to the behaviour of the parents.

Ms Burnley and Mr Fletcher
When Ms Burnley and Mr Fletcher's baby was just two weeks old, the health visitor became concerned about his not gaining weight. The midwife called round to weigh him, and dropped him. He was taken straight to hospital. 'They said I could have him back. I went to see him every day. He's never come back. They told my mam, "She cannot look after them".' A place of safety order was taken out and the baby was made a ward of court. When he was nearly six the court ruled he should be adopted. 'They was making me to have him adopted but I didn't want to. But I like went through it. I was carrying again. I said to them, if you take this one off me I'd just kill myself. I would though.' With support the couple have been able to raise their second son who is now two years old

and attending the local nursery. Of her first child, Ms Burnley says, 'I'm just waiting. I'm going to wait till he knocks on the door. You see, if I have him back I'll be a family, a proper family. He knows I'm his mam: his first mam and first dad.'

Ms Austin
Ms Austin was seventeen and living in a hostel for people with learning difficulties when she had her first baby. She had wanted to keep the child but while she was still pregnant social workers told her the baby would be removed at birth. She never saw him and didn't know if they had kept the name she had given him. This was three years before she met her present partner by whom she has two further children – Amy who is four years old and Tony who is three. 'I still miss him', she says.

Other parents experienced pressure from the family to let their child go.

Mrs Pollock
After Mrs Pollock's mother died on her sixteenth birthday, 'my dad had affair with me. I had a baby to him. They just said it depends what I do, you see, because it's with my dad's child. I can have him put away but I didn't want him to put away. I wanted to keep him myself. But my dad wanted to put away, you see, because then nobody won't know. My dad didn't want it. I had to sign papers to say I'd put him away. He weren't that old. A few weeks. I could've kept it. I could've brought it up myself.' Mrs Pollock has since married and is bringing up two boys.

Mrs Spencer
Mrs Spencer's first child was the result of rape. When she found she was pregnant she turned to her boyfriend, who was not the father, for help. After a long talk they decided the best thing to do was to get married. Doctors tried to dissuade him but they went ahead because they wanted to keep the child. 'I says what are you trying to make out she is? Even animals has their own young, I says.' As soon as her son was born, Mrs Spencer's parents intervened. They took her and the child home from hospital without telling Mr Spencer. Despite his vigorous protests, his wife and the baby remained at the grandparent's home. They would let neither of them have anything to do with the baby. Mrs Spencer was not even allowed to touch him. In a desperate bid to ease his wife's anguish, Mr Spencer contacted her social worker and asked her 'to take the child in care so Rosie can get back and be happy again'. He reasoned that once the baby was in a children's home they would be able to visit and pick up the child 'so she feels like a mother and I'll feel like a father'. Jonathan was a month old when he was taken into care. He remained until he was eighteen. He is now in his thirties with children of his own and maintains

regular contact with his mother. Mr and Mrs Spencer brought up two further children of their own.

3. *Parents who have had a child taken away while others were left in the family.*

The parents' inability to provide good-enough care was not the reason for the child being taken away in these cases. They continued to look after their other child(ren). Factors other than the lack of basic parenting skills precipitated the removal of the child from the family.

Mr and Mrs Derby
Mr and Mrs Derby have three children, Alan (aged 18), Ann (16) and Matthew (9). Mrs Derby has learning difficulties. When their daughter transferred to middle school she started to truant and keep company with a gang of girls who were always getting into trouble. Sometimes she would go missing for a day or two at a time. She also began to vandalize her own bedroom and exhibit an enuresis problem. Her father became convinced that she was caught up in a paedophile ring. 'They've been using this chap's house as a meeting point.' Fearing for her welfare, he kept her away from school and refused to allow her out of the house. 'I thought I can't stand it any longer. At least I'll have more peace of mind if I can see she's here.' Eventually the local Education Department took action and a social worker was attached to the family. Mr Derby expressed his fears to the social worker but Ann was finally taken into care and placed in a children's home after being accused (though never charged) with theft. 'You feel as though they're telling you you're inadequate as a parent. I mean there's about three or four girls involved with this sex thing, but how come our Ann always seems to be one that's put into a home? The other girl she was with, she's still at home. We saw her the other day, she wasn't at school.' Initially there was talk by social services of placing her with a foster family but Ann refused. After she had been in care for six months, Mr and Mrs Derby were informed that the review panel had decided to allow her to return home after her sixteenth birthday. They have recently moved house in the hope of making a fresh start away from her old friends. Ann has since had a baby by a young man she met in the children's home.

Mr and Mrs Hardy
It was only after they had married that Mr Hardy realized his wife had very little idea about how to run a home and look after their small son. He admits their house was a mess. When Simon was 22 months old the authorities decided that he wasn't thriving and was lacking stimulation. He was taken into care. At this time, Mrs Hardy was expecting a second child. She was advised by her social worker to have an abortion. Following the birth of their daughter, Mr Hardy was told that if he did not give up work to look after the baby then she, too, would be taken into care. He took over the running of the house and the care of the child, and also

began teaching his wife the skills she needs for coping. Initially they had access to Simon once a fortnight while he was with foster parents. When he was placed with prospective adoptive parents, access was eventually stopped altogether. In court, Mr and Mrs Hardy pleaded for his return home for a trial period so they could show how much things had altered for the better. 'I want him back home. I mean he'd get cared for, the same what Alice does. I mean you can see no problem with Alice there. If we can do it with one we can do it with another.' In his affidavit, their social worker acknowledged that the care provided by Mr Hardy for their baby daughter had been 'very good' and that he had shown 'commitment' and 'enthusiasm' for the task. However, he argued, Mr Hardy would not be able to maintain an adequate standard of care for another child given that his existing parental duties extended not only to his 18-month-old daughter but also to his wife. The court agreed to release Simon for adoption. Two years later Mrs Hardy became pregnant again.

4. *Parents who received no help or support with the problems that eventually precipitated the removal of their child(ren).*

In a review of the concomitants of parental adequacy, Tymchuk (1992) concludes that

> a significant predictor of the adequacy of the provision of health care and safety for a child of a person with mental retardation is the adequacy of the supports that person has regardless of their own level of knowledge and skill.

Yet as Czukar (1983) has pointed out, parents with learning difficulties are especially vulnerable to losing custody of their children because of lack of appropriate support services. Gilhool and Gran (1985) suggest one reason is the persistence among service providers of the misconception that because they learn more slowly and need more reinforcement they cannot learn at all.

Ms Richards
Ms Richards had been fostered by her aunt but she grew unhappy with the restrictions placed on her freedom. At 15 she ran away. Eventually she was placed in a hostel for people with learning difficulties. She became involved with a man who took advantage of her vulnerability and her feelings for him to exploit her sexually. In time, she found herself pregnant. 'I were really, really chuffed about it. I thought he might be too. I went up to him and told him I was pregnant and he said get rid of it.' She chose to see out her pregnancy. 'I was frightened all the way through but really looking forward to being a mum. I was living with this couple and they helped me, used to look after me. But things got a bit out of hand like, saying that I couldn't look after her and that I wasn't feeding her properly.'

She was taking feed but she kept on bringing it all back, and we had to take her to hospital because she were going blue in the face. She kept on getting sore and that, and we kept on bathing and bathing her, and we weren't letting her go mucky or owt like that, but I think it were like nappy rash having problems with. My social worker kept coming up to the house to see how everything were going and he asked me how I were coping. I said, well not too bad. This couple showed me how to deal with her but I think it were me. That like not being learnt in the early stages how to look after a child and that, I think that's what it was. We was shown this film about sex and that but I wasn't taught how to cope. If they'd have give me summat, like learn me, taught me how to look after a baby, I'd been all right.' Ms Richards' daughter has been adopted although she has regular access to her.

Ms Pointer

As a single parent, Ms Pointer received no help from the father of her child. 'My mother said have an abortion but I said no, I were going to have him.' She had spent much of her own childhood in residential homes although she kept in regular contact with her family. For the first three months after her son was born she lived with a couple who helped her look after him. She then moved back to her flat on the far side of the city away from her mother and sisters. 'It were when I went back to my old flat I couldn't cope. It were getting on top of me. He wouldn't stop crying and I accidently bruised his head. They took him into Children's Hospital. He stopped in there a week. Then my social worker took him into their care and I see him twice a week. She asked me who could look after him and I said my sister. I had to tell them in end that it were my fault. She didn't even bother to come and see me, my social worker. She come up like, she used to come up once a week. But she wouldn't listen to me. She's only young, social worker. I would have liked to have looked after him, if I had somebody near me what could help me like. But with living up other end of city it were too far for my family to come and see me.' Ms Pointer's son was just a year old when he went to live with her sister. She is allowed to take him out one day a week, and she sees him at her mother's home at weekends.

5. Parents who were compromised in their caretaking role by competence-inhibiting support.

Tucker and Johnson (1989) make a distinction between competence-promoting and competence-inhibiting forms of support (see also Chapter 5). Competence-promoting support allows the parents to feel in control while at the same time developing their caretaking skills. Competence-inhibiting support tends to be based on the assumption that the parents 'are incapable of managing on their own and that intervention is necessary for the child's sake'. It is generally unresponsive to the parents' own needs, denies them the opportunity of overcoming problems on their own, undermines their sense of self-worth and provides little motivation for them to improve their parenting skills. The effect is often to belittle the parents' own efforts and to cast their child care abilities in a purely negative light. Some parents in our study rejected what they saw as intrusive help delivered on the service provider's own terms and in so doing further prejudiced professionals' views of their fitness for parenthood.

Mr and Mrs Stewart

Mrs Stewart, who has learning difficulties, had always suffered from poor eyesight but, after the birth of her second child, she became totally blind. She lapsed into a severely depressed state. Mr Stewart saw his wife change: 'I swear it broke her.' He tried to cope with their two small children, his wife and a job. 'I coped for nine months on my own before I started getting a home help. When you're a man looking after children the health visitors keep a close bloomin' watch. They seem to pick on you more, and I felt as though they were ruling my life. We had a health visitor that was very domineering. She came that often it were like having a second bloomin' wife. She really did wear me down.' Mr Stewart began to receive visits from social workers 'checking to see everything's right'. 'They send kids of about 25, if that, not qualified, they might just be learning. They were giving me all this advice about children and I says to them, "Well, have you any children, love? Are you married?" I thought, they're trying to give me all this advice with no children. When you're bringing up children, and you're tired, you've to really experience it.' For the first twelve months, Mrs Stewart was in and out of hospital before she was found a place in a residential home for blind people nearly a hundred miles from her family. She stayed there for three months before returning home. 'I thought they were going to train her to do things in the home like, to make a cup of tea and that, but she came back just the same.' Over the years Mrs Stewart was tried in a variety of residential placements including a psychiatric hospital, and a hostel and long-stay hospital for people with learning difficulties. When at home she also attended an adult training centre and different community day centres. She remained withdrawn, however, and deteriorated further both mentally and physically. She even stopped talking. Mr Stewart feels that no one ever tried to help her to come to terms with the loss of her sight, or to move beyond assessment to rehabilitation. 'You see, these places that she's been to be assessed, she's only been doing basic things, like she does knitting and drawing. I think what they should have done at the beginning, she might be too old now and it might not just sink in, but if they'd spent twenty years trying to teach her such as brail. I thought they could have done something on that score because she was only young when she went blind.' For the past four years Mrs Stewart has been attending a special care unit for people with multiple and profound disabilities twice a week. Although not a suitable placement in many ways, it is the first time any attempt has been made to help her acquire practical living skills or to teach her how to make the most of her abilties. Mr Stewart has seen an enormous improvement in her manner and outlook on life. 'I says there's one thing that all these other places haven't got. There's a load of love there and they share it out equal.'

6. *Parents who lost their child(ren) because of the behaviour of a partner without learning difficulties or with additional problems.*

In these cases the children were put at risk by factors also associated with abuse and neglect in families where the parents do not have learning difficulties. The examples among the study families all involved cases where a parent had serious psychiatric problems (see also Mickelson 1947) but alcoholism or violent behaviour, for instance, would also fit into this category.

Mrs Redwood

Mrs Redwood has learning difficulties and a history of mental health problems. She met her husband in a long-stay psychiatric hospital where he had lived for many years. 'We moved out because I were expecting Barbara. I looked after her and then she started with poorly hips. I wanted to look after her, but they wouldn't let me. My husband was shouting when he come in. Shouting everywhere when he come in from pub and baby was in room. He used to hit me. They wanted her adopted. I didn't want that, I wanted to keep her.' Barbara was fostered by the grand-parents, with whom she has lived ever since. Mr and Mrs Redwood were divorced and he has since died.

Mr Gore

Mr Gore had a tormented childhood which has left him a legacy of mental health problems. He has been under a psychiatrist for some time. His wife has learning difficulties. When they married he wanted her two-year old daughter, the result of a rape, to remain with her grandparents but Mrs Gore insisted the baby live with them. They had two children of their own, a girl and a boy. Shortly after the birth of their youngest child Mr Gore was suspected of sexually molesting his stepdaughter and she was placed with foster parents. Subsequently, the second girl was also removed from the home. Mr Gore has a violent streak that has often led him into trouble. He has been ejected from a number of job schemes for getting into arguments and fighting. At home he has kicked holes in doors and ripped paper off the walls. He was taken to court for breaking an 11-year-old boy's nose and only escaped a custodial sentence because the judge was persuaded that Mrs Gore would not be capable of looking after the children without him at home. Their son also was eventually taken into care. According to Mrs Gore's sister: 'The government man says Gay done her best but Rick didn't act like a father should with the kids.' Finally he was found guilty of sexually interfering with a 14-year-old girl and sent to prison for nine months. They are now divorced. Mrs Gore has access only to their son.

7. *Parents whose children present management problems of a severity that would tax the coping abilities of any family.*

Mr and Mrs Baker
Mrs Baker has learning difficulties and her husband also attended special school. He works long hours as a machine fitter as well as being on call at night. They have two children, a boy aged five and a two-year-old daughter. Their son has learning difficulties and has been diagnosed as medically hyperactive. He frequently has disturbed nights. 'Two or three mornings, at night, he'll wake up and sit up in bed just screaming. And all you can do then is just go to him and comfort him. He might get up screaming at one o'clock in the morning and then at three o'clock he might be screaming again and he'll just sit there screaming in bed. I've come down here at half past five in the morning and I've heard him come down and he'll put telly on. He sleeps about five or six hours out of twelve. Out of seven nights he'll probably have three bad nights.' The Bakers were very keen for Phillip to go to a mainstream school but the teachers decided they couldn't manage him and he was sent to a special school. He also suffers from asthma. 'When he starts wheezing it's like a machine going off. He starts wheezing that much and then it takes him all his time to breathe.' A social worker once asked Mrs Baker how she coped with Phillip. She replied, 'The best way I can.'

Mr and Mrs Pollock
Mr and Mrs Pollock have learning difficulties and their two sons, Stewart, aged eight, and Justin, aged six, both go to special school. Mr Pollock has been suffering from clinical depression since the death of his mother a year ago. As a baby, Stewart was placed in foster care when social services decided his parents were not capable of looking after him. They managed to get him back after a year when their solicitor convinced the court that the best place for him was with his mum and dad. Since then they have had almost no help or support from social services. 'They always said that when your kids are growing up you can cope on your own.' Recently Stewart has been giving them problems. 'I went up to school to see one of head teachers. I told them that we couldn't cope with our Stewart because he was swearing and biting and saying these 'f' words like that. They can't find out what's happening. They've told him to behave himself at home but he never does. Might be his ways, they says, because he's getting older now.' The community nurse has told Mr and Mrs Pollock that Stewart may have to go into care full-time. They don't want that and neither does Stewart. She has also talked of Justin being taken into care as well but the Pollocks insist he is no problem. Their difficulties are seen as personal inadequacies rather than a result of the pressures of bringing up two growing boys with learning difficulties.

8. Parents whose children were removed as a precaution in anticipation of problems arising at a later date.

Mr and Mrs Armstrong

Mr and Mrs Armstrong have three children. Their eldest boy Mark, aged seven, was difficult to control from an early age. He was taken into care on a few occasions before being permanently fostered with Mr Armstrong's brother and his wife. 'He's quietened down now. I just wish I could've done for Mark as my family's done. I couldn't cope with Mark, and I feel bad about it.' Their second son Carl, aged four, was also very active and challenging. Social Services decided that 'Carl will get like Mark because he's following in his footsteps'. The Court ruled that both Carl and their daughter Kate, aged three, should be taken into care together. Kate was a talkative, well-behaved and friendly little girl who presented her parents with no problems. 'Mark was getting into a lot of trouble with other kids. Carl was a handful. But I'd have coped with Kate. I can't understand why they took Kate. She's well mannered, you know.' All three children now live separately with different foster parents.

Discussion

The material presented in this chapter corroborates and amplifies the view of Dowdney and Skuse (1993) that a child's reception into care is an unsatisfactory criterion of parental inadequacy in the case of people with learning difficulties. We have shown that the removal of children occurs for reasons other than parenting failure; that child care problems cannot be taken as an unambiguous sign of inadequate parenting; that children are placed in care for reasons other than their parents' learning difficulties; and that parental competence is no guarantee of parental rights. A number of variables have been identified that influence the relationship between parental adequacy and child outcomes, including professional prejudices and stereotypes, the attitudes of support workers, the involvement of grandparents and other members of the extended family, the quality and type of support provided, the social situation of the parents, the nature of the marital relationship, access to legal representation, children with special needs or behavioural problems and the presence of a spouse with (typically) mental health problems. These observations have implications for future research and professional practice.

Future research

Research on the quality of parenting provided by people with learning difficulties needs to be set in the context of their own lives and biographies. Such an approach is important as a check against four potential traps:

• *Judging or assessing parents against inappropriate standards of care.* For example, several study families reported having been warned against smacking their children. Ever fearful of losing them, they did as they were told. However, generally lacking powers of verbal reasoning, they were left with no effective method of discipline and began to encounter problems of control. These problems were then cited by social workers as evidence of parenting deficits. Or again, many parents were expected to maintain standards of household tidiness and cleanliness that were foreign to their neighbourhoods, family and friends, and unnecessary in terms of the health or well-being of their children. As Ms Burnley complained: 'They want me to get my house perfect but I cannot get it perfect. I'm not like other people, them posh people. It's just like other houses round here. With Tessa you've to wipe your feet when you come out.'

• *Focusing only on parenting deficits or failure and ignoring parental achievements and success.* Much of the literature on parents with learning difficulties is characterized by a 'deficiency orientation' (see Chapter 6) that has given more attention to parental inadequacies than to parental competencies. This has come about despite evidence that a substantial proportion of parents in fact provide adequate child care (Tymchuk and Keltner n.d.). The majority of children in this study were being raised at home by their own parents. Biographical methods can serve as a corrective to this form of selection bias by examining parents' experiences in the round. As Bogdan (1974) observes, they enable 'us to look at subjects as if they have a past with successes as well as failures, and a future with hopes and fears'.

• *Incorrectly ascribing inadequate child care or unsatisfactory child outcomes to parenting deficits.* Setting the specific child care problems of parents with learning difficulties in their wider family and social context enables the impact of environmental pressures and strains – such as poverty, unemployment, bad housing, harassment and victimization – to be more clearly identified. When Ms Austin agreed to sign over her children to her common-law husband it was not because she was unable to fulfil her role as a mother but because it offered a way of getting them out of the decrepit caravan in which they had been forced to live for a year and into a proper home from the priority housing list (see Chapter 6).

• *Oversimplifying people's lives and relationships.* Concepts like parental adequacy and parenting failure are summary descriptions of people's lived experience. There is a danger of using them to impose order and meaning on lives that are 'more ambiguous, more problematic and more chaotic in reality' (Faraday and Plummer 1979). The life story approach provides a way of clarifying such analytical categories and ensuring they are grounded in the real world.

Finally, research in this field needs to give more attention to the process of parenting by people with learning difficulties. During our intensive fieldwork with study families, we came across examples to support almost every well-documented generalization that has been made about the characteristics of their parenting behaviour, including: the failure to adjust parenting styles to changes in their child's development; a lack of verbal interaction with the child; insufficient cognitive stimulation, especially in the area of play; a tendency to overgeneralize instructions; inconsistent use of discipline (and, in particular, a reliance on punishment at the expense of praise); a lack of expressed warmth, love and affection in relationships; and a weakness for putting their own wants and needs before those of their children. At the same time, we also encountered examples (even within the same families) of behaviour that confounded every one of these points. The fact is that parents with learning difficulties do not constitute a homogeneous group with a shared lack of parenting skills. Yet research so far has given most weight to questions of central tendency: to exploring how such parents differ from parents without learning difficulties. There is a need for researchers to place more emphasis on their individual characteristics and to redirect their work towards acquiring a better understanding of why some parents succeed when others do not (Greenspan and Budd 1986).

Professional practice

Much professional practice is guided by the implicit belief that some minimum level of intellectual functioning is necessary for adequate parenting. As a result, children are removed from their families not because they receive inadequate care but because their parents have learning difficulties.

There is a constant tension between the 'policing' and the 'enabling' role of social workers. The 1989 Children Act has reinforced this split by bringing neglect as well as abuse under the purview of child protection teams. As a result, parents with learning difficulties are at risk of being referred for investigation under the 'duty to enquire' clause because the presumption of incompetence provides sufficient cause to suspect significant harm. At the same time, the danger of their being assessed as incompetent is heightened because the practitioners involved are now usually specialists in child protection work and have little or no experience in the learning difficulties field.

As Harris (1990) observes, families in difficulty 'typically turn to the very professionals who have the main statutory responsibility for child protection'. In their 'policing' role, practitioners are responsible for defining good-enough parenting and for determining if parents meet these standards. In their 'enabling' role, they command the resources with which to influence the outcome. The negative assumptions held by many practitioners about parents with learning difficulties combined with the deficiencies in the support services – especially the lack of any systematic training in parenting skills and the lack of adequate independent representation for parents – conspire to make action against the parents more likely. The approach often seems to be, 'I don't believe you can cope and I'm not going to give you the support to prove me wrong'.

The reasons for summary denial of the right of people with learning difficulties to bring up their own children are no more persuasive than in the case of other categories of people whose behaviour or condition might be detrimental to the well-being of their children such as alcoholics, drug abusers, people with mental health problems or low-income families (Petchesky 1979; Greenspan and Budd 1986). The key issue is the willingness and ability of parents to fulfil their parental duties and responsibilities, and these cannot always be determined in advance. At the same time, it will not do just to sit back and wait until they fail. People with learning difficulties are doubly disadvantaged in providing good-enough parenting by the legacy of discrimination that, among other things, denies them any preparation for parenthood (Madsen 1979). Parental rights should only be terminated after determined efforts have been made to remedy the parents' problems and these efforts have failed (Gilhool and Gran 1985). Without the resources and supports to enable them to bring up their children, the right of people with learning difficulties to become parents is a hollow badge of citizenship. The statutory services still have much to learn about how best they can secure and uphold the citizenship rights of parents with learning difficulties as well as protect the welfare of their children.

CHAPTER 5

The price of support

All the families in our study were receiving support of some kind from the statutory services. While recognizing they needed help in order to cope, they often complained bitterly about the terms on which it was delivered. Some paid dearly for what they got. Service workers and professionals occupied an ambivalent status in the lives of the parents. They were a valued source of support for some. For others they brought little but heartache and trouble. Mostly they were seen as a mixed blessing.

Using parents' comments and family outcomes as yardsticks, the following key features of good practice may be identified:

- workers with a genuine liking or feeling for the families concerned, who understand their point of view, are not seen as interfering and respect them as people;
- practical support that is sustained over the longer term and directed towards teaching, maintaining or reinforcing parents' own skills;
- recognition of the emotional needs of parents;
- the mobilization of community supports, including the extended family;
- close integration of formal services and informal support networks;
- independent advice or advocacy, especially in cases where the worker is unable to represent the interests of both the parents and the child.

The most common features of unsatisfactory practice, on the other hand, were as follows:

- inconsistency of treatment between different families or by different practitioners working with the same family;
- lack of continuity in service delivery and a high turnover of support workers;

- poor coordination and collaboration between different agencies and different workers;
- social workers with book knowledge only who lacked personal experience of parenting;
- failing to notice problems before a crisis erupts;
- usurping parents' authority in their own home;
- treating the parents as less than fully adult;
- failing to involve parents in decisions affecting their lives or to respond to parents' concerns;
- using parents' fears of losing their child to secure their acquiescence;
- meddling in matters that have no bearing on the reasons for intervention;
- judging parents by inappropriate standards and values;
- seeing parents and children as individuals, and diminishing the importance of their relationships;
- attributing deficits in the services to the inadequacies of the parents;
- taking advantage of people's learning difficulties.

This chapter focuses on just one of the couples in our study in order to illustrate some of these features of good and bad practice and how they impact on the lives of parents.

Julie Burnley and Neville Fletcher's story

Julie Burnley spent much of her childhood in residential schools and with foster parents ('They kept moving me every time I go to bed at night'). When she was 18 she met and fell in love with Neville Fletcher at an Easter Fayre at the social education centre he attended. Neville had lived with his mother until he was in his twenties. His father had died in a mining accident when he was 11, and his mother had raised him and his four brothers by herself. When he left home he lived in a hostel for a spell before he and his brother were given a flat. He gradually became 'fed up' with social workers calling on them and eventually moved in with a friend's mother. Both Julie and Neville have learning difficulties.

They had been courting for two years when Julie became pregnant. For a while she stayed in a homeless person's hostel, but after the birth of their son the council gave them a house and, when Julie came out of hospital, they moved in. Suddenly, Julie and Neville found themselves responsible for budgeting their money for food and clothes, paying the bills, preparing meals and cooking, washing and ironing, doing the shopping and keeping the house warm and clean. This was difficult enough without also having to adjust to living together and care for a new baby.

When their baby was just two weeks old, the health visitor became concerned about his not gaining weight. A midwife called round to weigh him, and dropped him (in front of witnesses). He was taken straight to hospital. Soon afterwards Julie and Neville were told he would not be returned to them. A place of safety order was taken out and he was made a ward of court.

There was a long delay of nearly two years between the baby's being warded and the date of the custody hearing. The court decided to leave him with foster parents on the grounds that Julie had no insight into the needs of a young child. Julie and Neville were allowed regular access. Julie was told she was being put on Depo-Provera injections: 'My mam said to a social worker, "Why can't Julie have any more?" and they told my mam, "She cannot look after them".' However, after a few years she began using the contraceptive pill. At some point she stopped taking it.

The issue of their son's adoption arose at the same time as Julie found herself pregnant again. He was nearly six when the court decided he should be released for adoption. Julie recalled: 'They was making me to have him adopted but I didn't want to, but I like went through it.' Thereafter, all contact between him and his parents ceased apart from a photo which Julie and Neville are sent once a year and the birthday and Christmas presents they are allowed to leave for him at the Social Services office. Julie and Neville had to accept they had lost him, at least for the time being. As Julie said: 'I'm just waiting. I'm going to wait till he knocks on the door, that's all. You see, if I have him back I'll be a family, a proper family. He knows I'm his mam: his first mam and first dad.'

They continued to nurse concerns for their son. On one occasion they had seen him in town with his new parents and his lip had been swollen. The adoptive parents told Julie that he had fallen off his bike. Julie was not so sure: 'I don't know if they're hitting him or not.'

Julie gave birth to a second boy, Jeremy. ('I said to them if you take this kid off me I'd just kill myself.') After Jeremy was born the Social Services and the community mental handicap team decided to draw up a visiting and support programme for the family. A social work assistant was introduced to Julie while she was still in hospital, and both parents took to her immediately. (As Julie said later: 'She's been all right with us. She's like a mam to us.')

The house the family lived in was on a run-down council estate smitten by telltale signs of vandalism, poverty and neglect such as boarded-up windows, overgrown gardens and broken fences. Support workers refused to visit at night, and the police had advised those attending the local women's group not to venture out alone after dark. Julie suffered a lot of abuse from local children ('They call me a gyppo; they call our Jeremy's not clean'). Occasionally they had a window smashed by stones or Julie would find her washing-line cut through. Sometimes she saw other women on the estate maltreating their children and could not understand why only she and Neville had been singled out to have social workers checking on them and their son taken away. ('Why've they took my kid off me, not Barbara's?') They were not happy living there.

When Jeremy was small, Julie and Neville had twice daily visits from support workers or community nurses. According to their social worker, these were intended to 'motivate' them. Neville would mix the feeds and do the feeding charts, while Julie fed the baby. As Jeremy grew older, checks were made on whether he had been fed the appropriate food for breakfast, on the state of the house, and to sort out their finances.

During the course of a week, five different workers would call at the house to check on the baby. All visits were recorded in a book kept in the living room. The entries were often derogatory in tone and praiseworthy comments were rare ('Julie was in a bad mood today and I had to tell her off for not hoovering the carpet'). Julie and Neville could not read their handwriting, and the book annoyed them intensely: 'If they keep writing in that book I'm going to put it back of the fire. I'm sick of seeing it. They're not me mam to make me do.'

They saw these visits as interference and a restriction on their independence. As Julie said on one occasion: 'I just want them to leave me alone, let me get on with my life. I don't want anybody telling me what to do. Only your mam should tell you off, not social workers. They treat me like I was one year old and I'm 26. I can't go out when I want cos I have to wait in for them. When I clean the place up for them they don't turn up.'

Julie and Neville felt themselves to be under constant criticism, although the baby was thriving and his needs always came first. A persistent fear was that Jeremy, too, would be removed if they failed to live up to the expectations of the authorities. Julie confessed to being frightened that he might still be taken away from her 'if I argue with social workers'. Her sister reinforced the point: 'Sometimes they say to her, "Your baby's not clean enough. If you don't clean him up, we'll have to take him off you."' Julie added defiantly, 'I tell you now, they're not taking him off me.'

Julie and Neville had always enjoyed going out during the day, meeting some of their friends or other members of their extended family. They still managed it most days – after their daily visit. Julie had a sister who attended the local social education centre and they saw each other regularly. She, too, had given birth to a baby boy who had been fostered.

On the advice of a social worker, Julie joined a women's group in town where, once a week, the women talked over their problems and gave each other support. All the women that attended were mothers and poor. They were also clients of Social Services. Run by social workers, the group sessions were held in a dilapidated building, also used as a youth club, covered in grime and graffiti. In winter it was cold enough inside to force the women to keep their coats on and their babies well wrapped up. There was a hole in the roof through which the rain leaked. Most of the seats and tables had been vandalized, the floor was dirty and the toilets a mess. Although Julie liked some of the women, she was very critical of the surroundings: 'I know it's not decent . . . and they tell us about cleanness!' Nevertheless, here she started to learn about bringing up a baby the same way most mothers do – by observation and by asking questions.

Julie and baby Jeremy also attended a family centre and Neville accompanied them. They looked forward to these afternoons and the staff gave them considerable practical support and encouragement. The Centre had a number of community functions but the purpose of their particular session was to bring together families who had difficulty fitting into larger mother and toddler groups. It was attended by couples with learning difficulties, single mothers and a few with postnatal depression. In contrast to where the women's group met, it was warm inside, clean, friendly, brightly decorated and with much to occupy the children. The staff's efforts to make the surroundings attractive showed they valued the people attending. They also made sure the time spent there was lots of fun. Julie and Neville have little social conversation and found it difficult to mix with the other parents and their children. Little Jeremy, however, had no such problem.

As time went on, the visits by support workers became more erratic. Some days Julie and Neville would be waiting but no one would call. For whatever reason, their minders failed to notice the huge debts they were accumulating until the court orders started rolling in.

People had spotted Julie and Neville's vulnerability and abused their good nature. Julie used a catalogue from which others would order and not pay for the goods. Neighbours borrowed money and equipment and failed to return or repay it. Their gas meter was broken into; other women made use of Julie's washing machine; distant relatives lodged with them without contributing to their keep. Even Julie's stepfather tapped them for loans. Eventually things caught up with them. They defaulted on their gas bill, were fined for not having a TV licence and had their TV and video repossessed.

Once the full scale of their financial problems was realized, a new programme of intensive support was drawn up using a 'core and cluster' team. This entailed one of three workers being present in the house five to seven hours a day, every day, including some evenings. The support workers set out to get Julie and Neville into a routine with Jeremy; to help them budget, cook and shop (with the accent on buying nutritious foods); to sort out the home and make sure the fire was lit; and to see they were aware of the hazards now that Jeremy was crawling. In time the team thought their hours in the home would be reduced. Julie and Neville were involved in all the decisions that had to be made, except one. Fat stains on the ceiling showed evidence of a few cooking fires and the chip pan was thrown into the dustbin. Having dealt competently with the fires, Neville complained strongly but without effect. Chips were off the menu.

Jeremy was now just one year old. He was placed with a childminder on Tuesdays while Julie, accompanied by her support worker, went dry skiing, tenpin bowling, swimming and ice skating. On Wednesdays, Neville attended the social education centre to work in the agricultural unit. He was pleased to be back again as he enjoyed seeing his old friends and said he had been bored at home. But he would have preferred a place on a job training scheme.

Meanwhile, arrangements were being made to find Julie and Neville a way out of their debts. Social Services owned a pair of semi-detached houses in the grounds of one of their old people's homes in the next town. Three young men with learning difficulties, one of them Neville's brother, occupied one house and the other was vacant. Julie and Neville were given the chance of living there for a very small rent, including gas and electricity, until they paid off their arrears. They were both anxious to move away from the council estate and agreed readily to the suggestion, although their old tenancy was kept on for a month in case they changed their minds. The house was fully furnished and centrally heated with a gas fire, in place of their present coal fire, and a telephone. They also liked the fact that one of the support workers and her family lived just up the road and would be available in emergencies.

Before they moved into their new home, some of the carpets were replaced and a new three-piece suite bought. A freezer was ordered and the support team applied for money to have the house redecorated. Most of the furniture and furnishings in their old house were tossed out. It was to be a new beginning.

Both Julie and Neville liked their three support workers. Shortly after moving in they went on a week's holiday with two of them to Butlins financed by the local Round Table. Julie had only ever had one holiday before, with her foster parents. The family of the support worker who lived close by had also become involved with them – visiting, babysitting occasionally and passing on toys, clothes and equipment.

Neville used to mention how the intrusion of support workers into their private life had caused problems between them. Julie used to get very upset by their always being there and, as he once put it, 'sulked a lot'. She no longer got angry. 'It's different now', she explained. The support workers are there 'because we need help'.

Three months after the move

Julie had stopped attending the family centre – it was too far away – and the women's group had closed down. A new childminder was being found for Jeremy. The house was immaculate and the garden kept tidy by the council. Julie is not one to enthuse and gave little sign of what she really thought about their new home. Neville, on the other hand, was quite adamant: 'You won't get me back down there. Even if Julie goes back, I'll stop here.'

Instead of spending money eating out in cafés as they once had, Julie and Neville were being shown how to prepare their own meals. In the home, Julie did the washing and Neville the ironing. Child care was mainly Julie's responsibility while Neville mopped, swept and hoovered the floors. Jeremy, a happy child, was just about walking and had begun to explore his surroundings with tireless energy. They had been told that he was no longer a ward of court.

Whenever the support workers were around, Julie and Neville seemed to look to them for prompting about what jobs needed doing, whether it was making a cup of coffee for visitors, ironing or stopping Jeremy from touching the record player. On their own, Julie and Neville did things when it suited them. At some point Julie's fiercely independent streak had dimmed and she had ceased to resist the tendency of the services to take over. From persistently expressing her desire before their move to 'manage on my own' and for 'social workers' to stop coming ('I want to get rid of them though. I don't like them being on my back. I don't know why they don't leave us two alone to get on with our life'), she had become much more passive and accepting. Both she and Neville had realized that in order to keep their little son they had to do as they were told.

The quality of life for Julie, Neville and Jeremy seemed to have improved, although new tensions in their relationship were beginning to emerge as a result of the focus and intensity of support going into the household. Their isolation was more evident than before. Jeremy, too, had reached an age when he was beginning to need more stimulation and supervision, and this was placing new demands on his parents.

Three months later

Staff had noticed that Julie was putting on weight and were concerned about the possibility of her being pregnant. She had been on Depo-Provera and had seen no periods for a while. She was also overdue for her next injection as nobody had reminded her to make an appointment. Julie herself felt she could not cope with another baby, 'with the midwife coming in every day again, no way'. She had been told to take a urine sample to hospital although she was sure she could not be pregnant. Putting on weight, she insisted, was the result of 'sitting in a lot and eating more. We haven't been having sex.' As the test showed a few days later, she was right.

On the family front, Julie's eldest sister had fallen out with her boyfriend and had been wanting to stay with them. Neville and Julie had refused to put her up, but the boyfriend and his mother had persisted in making threatening phone calls to the house and intimidating them by sitting on the wall outside. As a result, staff had resumed their evening visits. Julie was annoyed: 'Just when we've moved away from trouble she brings it with her. Staff're going to come again and I don't like it. In evening I've got my baby to myself and I like baby to myself. I like them here, yes, but I want them to leave us alone in peace like I used to before.' Fortunately, Julie's sister and boyfriend were soon reconciled.

According to Neville, they were not going out much any more as it was too far to walk into town. Julie, in any case, thought it was boring looking round shops when they had no money. They hadn't eaten out for a long time like they used to enjoy doing – except on a couple of occasions when staff had accompanied them. 'Every Tuesday we used to go out for meals but now we don't. They've stopped that now.' Money was being saved in a box in the kitchen and in a bank account. Julie and Neville knew it was necessary to save money to pay off their debts and to put towards things they needed, but they had almost no say over how much they saved or how much they spent. 'They said in that meeting before we moved – we were stood on us own when we went to that meeting – they said we're going to move you, we're going to come in and we're not going to take money off you. And what've they done? They've took money off us. I'm not bothering like. They've not took it off us but it goes in the cash box. They give us pocket money.'

Jeremy was off walking and his parents were very proud of his achievement. Nevertheless, Julie felt constrained by the routine staff had fixed for his bedtime and upset at having to share him with them. Some of her old anger had returned. 'Jeremy's to get to bed at right time, and all that, and bathing him six o'clock and put him to bed at seven. That's too early for him. He's sleeping in the afternoon, like all babies does, and if I put him to bed at seven he's not going to sleep. I can't settle him down in this house. Before he used to come to bed with us. He didn't have sleep in afternoon. Everybody's mauling him and he doesn't like it. That's why he's mangy on a night time. I have to make sure he goes to sleep first when he goes to bed, but I can't. He lies awake and he will not go. Every time you come down he cries.'

'I'm never involved with money and I'm never involved with him neither. He's not my kid now. They've taken over. I like them here but I don't like sharing kid with me though. I like him for myself like other mothers does. I'm getting laughed at. I haven't said anything. Bloomin' daren't.'

Jeremy went to a childminder for the day on Tuesdays. Julie liked this childminder very much, but staff had other designs and were planning to enter him in a playgroup. Julie was not keen on this idea. 'I don't want him to go to the play school. They've been talking about it on Tuesday in their meeting and I don't want him to go to play school yet. I just keep my mouth shut. It's my kid, they're telling me what to do with him. I know what they do if there's kids older than him, they might hit him at that age. He's not going and I shall tell them he's not going. It's all right if I go with him, yes, but not on his own. I'm still scared if he has cot death at that age.'

At one time staff would accompany Julie and Neville when they did their shopping but now they went on their own. They were given money to buy food 'and then we have to put what's over back in the box. We're not allowed to take baby out to shop with us. They say it's too far to go there and with shopping bag and we'd got him. But all mothers does it.'

Staff had also changed their diet and not always to Julie and Neville's liking. 'We no used to eat meat at all, and we no used to eat cabbage, no used to eat carrots, fresh carrots. Used to eat them in the tin. They've got us eating meat, and I don't even like meat. We used to have chips sometimes, we used to have chicken. I like chicken.'

Almost a year after the move

Jeremy was now going to the childminder twice a week and Julie had enrolled two days a week at a further education college to learn cookery and English. She had learnt to write a few words and had done some simple arithmetic. Neville was hoping to have another day a week at the social education centre. Support workers had stopped coming in the evening as Julie and Neville had assured them that Jeremy was in bed by seven. They had been unable to find a babysitter to allow them a night out together.

While they did not want to move back to their old estate, Neville said they were thinking of putting their names down for another house. 'It's miserable around here.' They had few friends and although Neville would take himself to the local pub occasionally he knew no one there. They had recently been on a weekend trip by car to Carlisle with Neville's brother to visit his mother and they hoped they could do it again soon.

A month later

Jeremy's second birthday, and Julie had baked him a cake. She had also made their Christmas cake this year in her cookery class. She now caught the bus to college where she would often sit with a fellow student who lived close by. Occasionally she would be given a lift home by another neighbour.

Instead of watching television for relaxation, Julie had acquired a new hobby – jigsaws. They had bought themselves a second-hand music centre and enjoyed listening to tapes. Neville had been given a camera for Christmas and both he and Julie were pleased with their album of photos, mainly of Jeremy. Neville said he still missed going out in the evening for a drink with his friends, although he took himself to the pub once a month and occasionally to the pictures. They were still unable to go out in the evening together.

Jeremy had moved out of his cot into a bed and had begun attending a nursery two days a week instead of the childminder's. Neville and Julie were a bit upset because he had cried when they left him. Neville seemed more involved with Jeremy and said he spent the evenings playing with him, especially when he would not settle down and go to sleep.

All their outstanding debts had been paid off and they were currently saving for some furniture of their own. Julie said the Social Services house did not really feel like it was their home and they had put their names down for a council house. Their support workers had promised to take them to the seaside for a weekend in the summer and they were both looking forward to the break.

After finding out that his brother next door was buying oven chips Neville had asked a support worker if he and Julie could have them too. He added triumphantly: 'We're allowed to now. We won that one anyway.'

Audit and practice implications

Julie Burnley and Neville Fletcher's story has been recounted because it highlights many of the common themes and issues that emerge over and over again in the accounts and experiences of other families. It also shows some of the strengths and weaknesses of current service responses to parents like them, the inhibiting as well as the enabling character of the support offered, and the importance of the values and attitudes that practitioners bring to their work. For this reason, it is instructive to undertake a 'practice audit' of their case.

Tucker and Johnson (1989) provide a useful starting point for such an exercise. Adapting their ideas slightly for our purpose, they suggest that environmental strain (caused by poverty, bad housing, illness, personal crises etc.) influences the support system's perception of parental competence which in turn has a direct impact on the type and level of social

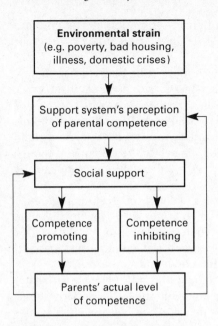

Figure 1   A model of parenting and social support

N.B. Environmental strains may also exert a direct impact on the social support parents receive (for example, where illness or death in the extended family robs them of a benefactor) and on the actual level of parental competence (as in the case of Molly Austin in Chapter 6). As this chapter is concerned solely with current service responses to parenting, these linkages have been omitted from the diagram.

support provided to families. Such support may vary from competence-promoting to competence-inhibiting in character. Competence-promoting support tends to allow parents to feel in control, to encourage them to handle their problems on their own, and to reinforce and develop their skills and sense of self-worth. Competence-inhibiting support is based on the assumption that the parents are incapable of managing on their own and tends to be demotivating, crisis-orientated, and unresponsive to the parents' view of their needs. All these factors have a bearing on the parents' actual level of competence which itself then loops back to affect how they are perceived by the support system. Figure 1 presents a flow chart of this model.

Applying this model to Julie and Neville's case produces the following 'practice audit'. One caveat should be mentioned. Their situation has not stood still. The move into new accommodation brought big changes in their lives, not all of them for the better. By the time our contact with them ceased their circumstances had changed again and they were looking to a new future. The practice audit spans the period covered by the story as told. Not all the factors listed under each of the headings below were necessarily present all the time.

Environmental strains

Among the pressures that have made parenting more difficult for Julie and Neville are:

● segregated and inadequate education, including lack of teaching in life skills;
● socialization deficits resulting from a childhood spent mostly in institutional care and providing little experience of family life or lacking parenting models;
● victimization in a poor neighbourhood;
● poverty and deprivation;
● the crippling effects of debt;
● poor housing on an impersonal estate, loss of tenancy and own home;
● little practical support from extended family or neighbours;
● problems in relationships with extended family members;
● long periods without respite from the daily grind;
● social isolation and harassment;
● no phone or immediate transport.

Perceptions of parental competence

The services and support provided for the family have revealed:

● a tendency to assume too easily that all problems were caused by the parents' learning difficulties;
● too little acknowledgment of the impact of environmental factors on the parents' coping skills;
● an assumed lack of nurturing skills, coupled with too little acknowledgment of the parents' capacity for learning (evidenced by the removal of their first child when only two weeks old);
● judgements about the adequacy of homemaking and parenting informed by inappropriate comparisons with middle-class norms;
● inadequate recognition of the emotional bonding between parents and child, and the trauma of separation;
● an undervaluation of the parents as people (illustrated by workers who failed to turn up when expected and services that diminished rather than enhanced their self-esteem);

- a readiness to consider the needs of the (second) child within the context of the family unit;
- a genuine liking for the family on the part of support workers;
- a belief in the family as warranting intensive support.

Competence-inhibiting support

Controlling features of the support provided to Julie and Neville were:

- manipulation of the parents' ever-present fear that their child might be taken away in order to ensure their compliance;
- absence of an independent complaints procedure or advocacy support, making it harder for the parents to assert themselves;
- a level of day-to-day surveillance that undermined the parents' independence and fostered their feelings of inadequacy;
- the intrusive staff presence and loss of privacy that stunted ordinary family life;
- lack of control over the comings and goings of staff;
- enforced dependence on staff for practical help and social needs that deskilled the parents;
- a reluctance on the part of staff to involve the parents in decisions about the care of their child and a tendency to impose their own views in matters of household routine such as bedtimes, cleaning, shopping and diet;
- failure to provide counselling to assist the parents in coping with the emotionally disabling loss of their first child;
- hit-and-miss supervision (which, for example, allowed them to build up large debts and led to a missed appointment for a contraceptive injection);
- use of segregated facilities (Social Services house and social education centre) that cut them off from the wider community and made them feel different from other families.

Competence-promoting support

Enabling features of the service response were:

- intense support given at crisis point;
- necessary and appropriate long-term practical support offered and maintained;
- practical training opportunities given, leading to self-reliance;
- grants applied for and received for furniture, furnishings and domestic equipment;

- a comprehensive check made on social security benefits available to the family (including exemption from poll tax);
- holiday arrangements made and family support maintained in unfamiliar surroundings;
- day care for child;
- practical help for coping with debts;
- introduction to family centre;
- introduction to women's group;
- stress eased by second child no longer being a ward of court;
- advice given on healthy diet;
- provision of nearby help in case of emergencies enhanced the parents' sense of security.

Actual level of parental competence

The parents have shown over the past six years:

- the capacity to function as a family unit with complementary skills – sharing the load in caring for the child, cooking, cleaning, shopping, ironing, etc;
- the capacity to recognize their own skills and their lack of them, and the ability to learn new ones with appropriate training;
- the ability to learn about childrearing from other mothers and fathers by observation and by asking questions;
- the ability to learn skills by example from support workers;
- the ability to form close loving relationships;
- the ability to maintain relationships under pressure;
- the capacity to put their child's needs before their own;
- an insight and awareness into the health and safety needs of a young child;
- a continuing concern and love for their first child and the strength of this parent–child bonding;
- the ability to learn (friendship, practical skills, child care) from community groups;
- a willingness to accept support in the home even though it is sometimes seen as an intrusion and a limitation on their independence;
- a sense of identity as a family.

Conclusions

Julie and Neville have lived much of their lives in segregated settings cut off from the opportunities for learning that come with participation in mainstream society. They have always been poor. Their problems as parents cannot be separated from these facts of life. At the same time, they have shown that with the right kind of support they can shoulder new responsibilities. The challenge for the support services and for practitioners is to ensure that they promote rather than inhibit such competence in parents like Julie and Neville. Although each case must be assessed on its own merits, there are ways of consolidating parents' hold on their future:

• By reducing the problems that cause stress. Support workers can give help with: money management; reading letters and filling in forms; emotional traumas; fear of losing their child; counselling for abuse or harassment; rehousing; advice on birth control methods to allow choice.
• By addressing problems caused by debt, lack of money and poverty of resources. Practitioners can help by explaining the benefits system, ensuring the family secure their entitlement, advising on budgeting and the use of money, applying for grants covering equipment, furnishings, clothes and shoes. Holidays and short breaks are also a necessity for most people.
• By improving access to resources such as: Family Planning Clinics; Relate; Samaritans; CAB; a crisis volunteer or telephone number; adult education; leisure and sports outlets; respite; babysitting services; skill acquisition sessions; self-help groups and community networks; employment opportunities; and, if possible, other parents in the same position.
• By looking into the possibility of linking the parents with another family to learn the art of childrearing – someone from the local church may choose to get involved – or introducing them to an existing family support or mothers' group.
• By encouraging health awareness and explaining the importance of regular visits by all the family to their GP, dentist and optician.
• By seeking to affirm parents' identity as members of the community through the use of ordinary services and facilities.
• By reducing the number of practitioners involved with any one family. Three is enough to provide back-up for the family and workers alike. It is important to have support workers who are sympathetic with the family's particular needs, and who promote people's abilities without losing sight of their limitations. It is also important that support workers and families who spend so long in each other's company should actually like one another.

By building on their strengths, parents too can be made to feel good about their achievements and are more likely to accept help and advice. Julie Burnley and Neville Fletcher were lucky. Very few parents with learning difficulties are given a second chance.

CHAPTER 6

Living with Molly Austin

Molly Austin was one of the parents in our study. She is neither typical nor unique. Her story reveals many of the same threads as run through the stories of other parents – poverty, debt, poor housing, social isolation, lack of support, a disadvantaged childhood, abuse and victimization, the absence of good parenting models, shortcomings in the health and welfare services – but they are woven into the pattern of her own life. It also shows that, in common with the other mothers and fathers in our study, her competence as a parent may be seen in either a positive or a negative light depending on the position of the observer. We have already seen in Chapter 5 how practitioners' perceptions of parental competence can influence the kind of support provided to parents and, ultimately, family outcomes. Using a profile of Molly Austin, this chapter illustrates how the same raw material can be read in two contrasting ways, each of which leads to a different appreciation of her achievements, a different assessment of her needs and a different vision of her future. Any other parent's story could have served the same purpose. Molly stands for them all.

Mount and Zwernik (1988) distinguish what they call a 'deficiency orientation' from a 'capacity perspective' on individual planning and service delivery for people with learning difficulties. A 'deficiency orientation' concentrates on people's deficits and describes them in terms of their problems and limitations. By contrast, a 'capacity perspective' emphasizes people's positive qualities and builds on the strengths and abilities shown through their own life experience. Molly Austin's story highlights the differences between these two ways of thinking and demonstrates how a 'capacity perspective' can help to provide a deeper insight into her present situation and a more positive outlook on her life.

The personal profile given here is based on the kind of information an experienced practitioner might expect to acquire from intensive, long-term involvement with Molly and her partner Kevin Whittaker. It draws on twelve personal interviews with the couple (each averaging 75 minutes) and careful observation during visits spread over a period of 14 months. Two features of the profile should be highlighted. Molly's own voice is not prominent. This is partly because of her reticence in talking freely in front of a tape recorder (hence more of what she had to say came in unrecorded conversations and is given in reported speech or straightforward narrative), partly because there were areas of her life she chose not to discuss openly, and partly, too, because of a lack of fluency associated with her learning difficulties. In contrast, Kevin's views and opinions are expressed at length and come over with some force. He talked unselfconsciously when recording was under way, ranging over topics Molly did not mention and paying more attention to what he saw as the skills she lacks than the qualities she possesses. This sort of imbalance is something that any practitioner or researcher can expect to encounter – and must be wary of – in relationships where only one partner has learning difficulties.

A profile of Molly Austin

Molly and Kevin have been together for six years. Kevin used to be in the army and then had a series of jobs as a painter-decorator and a security guard. He now suffers chronic disc trouble and is waiting to be registered as disabled. Molly has learning difficulties. They have two children, Amy who is four years old and Tony who is three.

Molly and Kevin live on a run-down caravan site at the end of a half-mile, pitted dirt track. The only facilities are a communal shower block and a launderette. The store and social centre were vandalized so often they were shut down long ago. A mobile shop visits once a day. Police swoops are common and social workers only visit in pairs. Toys left outside are stolen.

Their caravan is damp and draughty. The one bedroom is unusable in winter and clothes left in it quickly mildew. Molly and Kevin sleep in the living room, while the children bed down in the dining area. Just now they are waiting for the site owner to mend a broken gas pipe and their only heating is a small electric fire. Last Christmas the water pipes had frozen and the whole family had to stay with friends in a one-bedroom flat.

When their children were babies Molly lived in a council house and Kevin took a job in London for a year. He had asked Social Services to keep an eye on Molly and to make sure she paid the rent every week with the money he sent her. Social Services said they would do this but nobody ever

called to check. When Kevin returned he found that Molly had accumulated huge rent arrears and, shortly afterwards, they split up. Kevin took
the children. After various temporary homes he and the children were
placed on the caravan site and, following intervention by a social worker,
Molly agreed to move in with them. They are now trapped on the site by
Molly's rent arrears and will not be considered for another council house
until the debt is cleared.

October to January

The caravan door is open because the children are playing outside. Inside it
is cold and Molly is well wrapped up. She comments on the dangerous
position of the gas cooker by the door where the children might knock the
pots off or the wind blow out the burners. She shrugs and brews a pot of
tea.

'We met at one of them unemployment [drop-in] places. We were out of
work so that were only place we could go. I've had a few jobs but they've
only been for a couple of months and that were it. I worked in an old people's
home, I enjoyed that. Helping old people, helping with dinners and washing
up and stuff like that. I got that when I were in children's home. We come
over this way cos his mother lives up here and she's not all that well.'

'We left that [council] house and then straight on to here and we had a
caravan up at top. Kevin asked if we could move into another caravan
because that one were falling to pieces, it'd got a big hole in it, so they give us
this one. It's cold in that bedroom so we put kids in here. We usually have a
little fire on which keeps this bit warm.'

'This is all my washing. I do it, or go to the launderette up at top. But it's 50
pence for chuffing washing, and it's 70 pence a time for drying them. So you
might as well save money and do your own washing. I only wash bits I really
need.'

'With Amy I was in hospital about a week, just to get used to her and that
and with Tony I stopped in a fortnight because they didn't trust me with him.
The kids were under care, they were under Social Services. Being in a home
and all that lot, they didn't think I could look after them myself. But they
don't bother now. Just the community nurse comes now and again.'

'Community nurse doesn't interfere. She just says how're you getting on,
that's all. It's just for file, just to make sure we're all right and kids are all
right. That's the reason why they come, to make sure they're all right. If I
have problems I just say can I have a talk with you, when she come, and she'll
say yes if you like, and I'd have ten minutes or something like that with her.
And sometimes she'll say, you're better off doing it that way instead of this
way.'

'If we've any problems they're there to help and that's it. But I haven't seen
them for nearly three month now because she keeps saying one of them's

sick or whatever, because she hasn't got a car and other one has. That's what she keeps saying. Social worker started coming and when she found out that community nurse were connected with us she said, "I won't bother coming now", she says, "because they're better off than me." You can't talk to social workers anyway, they're always changing.'

April

Molly has gone shopping with the children. Kevin is outside repairing a blocked drain. He stops work to make a cup of tea and talk.

'She left me. She's only been back three week. I've no idea where she went. When I've asked her she just says here, there and everywhere. It were on a Sunday. I'd just started preparing dinner and she just got up, packed some clothes, went. Never said tarra, I want to be on my own, or nowt. It's about fourth time she's left me. Well, this time the community nurse had a word with her. I don't know where they found her. They asked her to come back to me.'

'They come and asked me first. I says, well I don't know. She's here for three month, I says, and then she's off for a week or two week, then she's wanting to come back as if nowt's happened and then she's off again. I says I can't hope to keep a job down. As a one parent I get £65 a week.'

'According to community nurse, she was sick of this place. I said so am I. I says, I don't like it but I'm having to put up with it. Without Molly I could have a house for me and t' two kids. What do I do? Do I turn round to her, kick her out and say I can get a house, bugger you? Or do I say are you going to pay your rent arrears off so we can live together as a family? I can't make my mind up. I don't want to push her away. She's their mother; kids've got to have mother. I said if I want house for just me and two kids she can come visiting for three times a week but that's all. She can't stop overnight or nowt else as they'd be coming up and checking.'

'When she came back she were happy for about three days. She'd clean up and wash up after every meal and that. Then she went back to normal, right moody, snaps at kids all time, snaps at me. She's on about she wants to go again, leave. Because she's fed up. I mean she were moaning because she'd got kids all time and when I had them the community nurses got me a day care for two days a week which I keep up. But again, you see, with it being thick fog and that, Molly didn't fancy walking it today.'

'She's always had problems with kids. She's all right to play with them but for owt else she's got to be told everything. Even when Amy were a baby she were just slapping bottle in and just not looking. She sat like that watching box instead of watching baby and I used to do it. When I were at work like, midwife and health visitor used to come and they used to get somebody coming in every day to feed baby when I were at work and I'd take over at night time. She won't think for herself. At washing, she hardly washes them. I have to tell her to.'

'I've no idea about Molly's childhood. She won't speak to me about it. I got told her mother died giving birth to one of t' kids and the father were fetching them up and he abused them or summat and they got put into care. He never bothered with them again.'

'She always talks about being abused when she's having an argument with me. Her sister says she was raped by one of her boyfriends, this lad she were going with. She told me that she's had a kid and Social Services took it off her when he were born straightaway. She never even saw it. I think she were about seventeen.'

'I got told she was in a hostel on Canterbury Road and what they did was they had their own rooms, they'd to make their beds. There was a washer and a dryer and all they had to do was slap their stuff in and staff did rest, meals, the lot. Shopping, staff used to take them in car to post office, get their money, take them down town shopping, fetch them back. I think she must have liked it when they bloody did everything for her. If she didn't feel like shopping, or wanted to sit in and watch telly, staff'd do their shopping. Whereas me, I'd make them go out and do it. I don't know how long she was there. When I met her she'd just got her own flat and staff were coming every day to make sure she'd got food in and she were paying her rent.'

'She said she didn't want any kids and I said, well, I want some. And then next thing I know she says, I'm pregnant, I want to get rid. I says well, you get rid and you don't come back to me because I want it. So she had it, says she had it for me.'

'She were all right before she had Amy. She'd get up, do housework, go out and do shopping. But as soon as Amy came on scene that were it, she altered. Started getting right moody all time, snapping because she couldn't watch telly when she wanted or go to bed when she wanted, get up when she wanted. That's her ideal world, she's even said it herself.'

'I don't watch that much telly. I mean when our Tony comes in he'll put it on for cartoons. She'll watch them. I say to her make a cup of tea, "I can't, I'm watching these cartoons first". So I have to get up and do it missen.'

'Amy were a big change for her. I think in a way she were delighted with Tony. Tony can't do no wrong for her. If owt goes wrong Amy gets a good hiding even if Tony's done it. I mean this morning, our Amy wanted to give her a hug, "No, get away". Now if Tony did it, yes. She favours Tony, I don't know why.'

'She hasn't got the patience. They say, "Can I have some toys out, dad?". She says, "Don't you leave them all over the bloody floor". I says, "Hey, you were a kid once, didn't you have toys, get them all out?". She says, "No". I says, "Well that's your tough luck". That's when we have us arguments.'

'They were both unplanned. Well, I tried to plan them but she didn't, she didn't want to. She were supposed to go to doctor's every three month for needle. She never went, she went twice. She said she tried the pill and it made her bad. She tried that coil and that kept dropping out, so she says. They said the only thing left was the injection. She isn't using owt now but I'm not bothered. She says she couldn't cope with another one.'

'When I were working down London it got to the stage where Social

Services were going to take Amy into care. We'd just got Amy, she were about ready to have Tony. They turned round and said if you don't come home to help look after kids we're going to take them into care. So I had to work my notice, come back and just stop at home. That's what she wants. She doesn't want me to work, she wants me to stop at home all time. But she knows I get bored and fed up and that's when arguments start.'

'I was coming home from London for a week's holiday every three month and I asked if everything were all right, if she were coping, paying rent all right. It got up to £735 I think it was, and that's when I blew my top.

'They took Amy off her once and they give her straight to my mother. My mam said she'd look after her because I were due for my week's leave. She had no food in the house, that's why they took Amy off her. Well, I'd asked my mam to pop round everyday like, to make sure she were feeding and that, and my mam says what're you doing them for dinner or summat and she went in t'cupboard and it were just bare. So she took them down to her house, fed them and got in touch with Social Services. Because that time they used to do loans, and my mam says can you give her a loan. And they went round and that were it. They turned round and said are you prepared to keep her and feed her while we sort her out, and my mam says yes. She had her for about three week. I come home to find out that if I didn't stop at home to help look after kids they'd be in care. I were clocking £400 a week up, that were after tax. Molly come down for a weekend once, but she didn't like it she said. Me, I prefer it down there than up here.'

'As for help, I think she needs it in everything but she won't ask for it. She said once that she'd show herself up if she asked for it. I said, but if you don't ask that's when we don't know, and that's when the problems start. I have to tell her everything, she just won't think for herself. But when you're having to tell her everything she jumps on you.'

'I do a lot of the cooking. She's all right with chips, beans and sausage. But you know, cakes and buns and that, they're that hard you can throw them across wall and they bounce off at you.'

'She's buys comic things so she can look at pictures. When I said well, why don't you ask somebody for help if you can't read or write, she said "No, I'm scared". The trouble is she won't admit it and let people help her. I got a load of books with big print, easy for kids to read. I thought, well, if she reads to Amy and Tony, it's learning her to read as well. But no, she won't. Our Amy reads to me. All Molly does is looks at pictures. That's no good.'

'Community nurses got her into reading and writing in town. There were a woman going to teach her that way one-to-one. She went three times because community nurse were taking her, picking her up and taking her up. She went three weeks. As soon as community nurse says you can make your own way, she never bothered. She just wants the attention all the time.'

'She's all right while somebody's with a car and will take her and hold her hand. I've no intentions of doing that. I says you can expect it for Amy and Tony, but for her no way. She's big enough to do it herself. It's like what the community nurses says. They can't give all their time to her.'

'I've asked community nurse to test her on money, to go with her or summat to see. Personally I don't think she knows the value. According to her sister she's only got this far because of people helping her.'

'She's supposed to be on that invalidity. Now I've asked her why she was on that. She's no idea. I says you must know. Then she come out with, "I suffer with fits". She's never had a fit while I've been with her. I've asked community nurse but they can't say nowt until Molly says summat to them because it's all down in her file. She won't tell them to tell me what's wrong with her. She gets a sick note every year from doctor. As soon as she gets it she's straight down to social with it. She gets them to fill it in for her.'

'She can't and she won't ask for help. It's not easy, but I mean when people turn round and say we'll help you as much as we can and you just don't bloody bother asking, then there's summat wrong somewhere, isn't there?'

June

Molly and Kevin are now living in a slightly larger caravan as the floor had rotted through on their last one. When asked if she felt better for the move, Molly made no comment. They have recently been given an old twin-tub washing machine which Molly uses out on the grass as there is no room for it inside. Kevin had found some blankets in an abandoned caravan on the site and Molly is going to wash them and store them away for winter. The children were busy bringing out bags full of washing and already Molly had their coats hanging on the line.

Although the children are getting older and Tony is now out of nappies, Molly says she doesn't find them any easier. Kevin is wanting Molly to sign over responsibility for the children to him as, he says, he would stand a better chance of getting a house for them.

Amy is starting infants' school in September and Tony will have a place at the nearby nursery during the mornings. Both the school and the nursery are a twenty-minute walk away across the fields. At present, day care has been reduced to one day a week for each child.

August

Another warm day and Amy and Tony were outside on the grass doing acrobatics. Molly was inside the caravan listening to their new stereo system given by Kevin's mum. One of the straps on Amy's sandals had come unstuck under the foot and Molly was making a good job of sewing it back together. She still hates being in the caravan, especially when it rains heavily as the noise gets on her nerves. She mentioned that most people on the site are in arrears from their previous tenancy and, like her, are unable to rent another council house until they have paid off what they owe. She is thinking of seeing a solicitor about signing over responsibility for the children to Kevin so he can get priority housing as a single parent. Molly hasn't seen the community nurses for some time now.

She might keep on the caravan for herself and have the children at weekends; or again she might move into the new house after they'd got settled. She wouldn't like only seeing the children at weekends, but felt there's little else she can do. She didn't really feel anything for Kevin anymore. When she left him it was only the children that had brought her back. She is wanting to buy a camera to take their photos. The only ones she has were taken two years ago.

October

A dull, cold day, 11.45 a.m. The curtains of the caravan were drawn shut. Inside it was dark. Amy, lying on the settee, was away from school with a cold and Tony and Molly were sitting next to her. Kevin, who had suffered a recurrence of his back trouble, was sitting rigidly upright in a chair. All four were watching *Robocop* on video. The doctor had just that morning told Kevin he wouldn't work again. He had prescribed some cream for Molly to rub on Kevin's back, and diazepam.

The previous week the community nurse had taken Molly to a solicitor at her request for advice about assigning parental responsibility for the children to Kevin. In the event Molly had refused to sign the agreement form.

Tony will be starting at the nursery near Amy's school in November for two hours a day from 9.00 a.m. until 11.00 a.m. This means that Molly will have to walk to school and back three times a day. Six journeys of twenty minutes each is a daunting prospect every day, especially with winter coming.

November

A neighbour from their old estate had called to see them but Kevin had already gone out to collect his benefit money and to sort out the costs of moving. Having so little in the caravan, he will have to buy new furniture for the house. He is not eligible for a grant so he has been advised to apply for a loan. At present Molly feels that she and Kevin are getting along quite well. She likes him being at home.

For the first time Molly speaks of the baby boy she had when living in the Canterbury Road hostel. She had named him after her youngest brother and had wanted to keep him but he was taken from her at birth. She didn't know whether they had kept the name she had given him. This was why she had felt pleased when Tony was born and why he was her favourite. But she still missed her first son.

Kevin has chosen to be rehoused in the area near Amy's school and Molly is pleased that she will not be unsettled by having to change school. Molly reckons that frequent changes of school in her own childhood are why she herself has problems with reading and writing. She knows some words and can tell the time by her watch. She also says that understanding the value of money is not a problem. Her difficulties arise when trying to add a number of items up and work out the overall cost. She tries to cope by shopping in stores which give till receipts showing the amount tendered and the change due.

Molly has learnt that it will take her another five years to pay off her arrears at £2 a week. She had been told by the community nurse that she must make up her mind soon about the children. She has decided to let Kevin have them so they can have a proper home. She knows that she will not be allowed to visit the house under Kevin's benefit rules more than three times a week. She will stay on in the caravan. A court hearing has been arranged shortly to settle the issue of a residence order although Molly says it will be over in ten minutes. She has already signed the necessary form.

The 'deficiency' and 'capacity' perspectives

Molly feels she can only secure a decent home for her children by letting them go. It is easy to see her grim predicament as the result of her own lack of competence.

A deficiency perspective

The rent arrears that Molly accumulated while Kevin was working in London are the main cause of their present plight. They precipitated the initial break-up of the family, the loss of their council house and their move to the caravan site. Molly's inability to manage a household budget or maintain a domestic routine – illustrated by the empty larder, the need for her mother-in-law to take over caring for Amy until Kevin was able to return home, and her lack of everyday skills such as cooking – are detrimental to the welfare of the children and an underlying reason why they are trapped on the caravan site. Because Kevin cannot hold down a job with Molly needing him at home, the family is condemned to subsistence on social security with no immediate prospect of paying off her debts.

Moreover, Molly appears incapable of living up to her responsibilities as a mother or of putting her children's needs before her own. Indeed, she had not wanted children in the first place. She fails to keep them clean or provide an adequate diet. She is unable to provide them with sufficient cognitive stimulation, especially in the areas of play, language development and reading. If left to herself, she would get up and go to bed when she wanted and spend the day watching TV. She is inconsistent and punitive in her use of discipline. There is an absence of expressed warmth, love and affection in her relationships and a lack of commitment to the family as a unit. She says she feels nothing for Kevin and she has walked out on the family without warning for weeks at a time on several occasions.

Molly has shown herself to be incapable of asking for help or of accepting it when offered. She rebuffed Kevin's efforts to encourage her to read, and withdrew from adult education classes arranged by the community nurses when they stopped giving her a lift and she had to find her own way there and back. She resents having to take the children to day care. She has never taken contraception or family planning seriously – even failing to keep appointments with her doctor for Depo-Provera injections – and currently is taking no precautions at all. Although in need of a lot of support, she denies the fact and seeks to cover up her deficiencies – even keeping from Kevin the reason why she gets invalidity benefit.

Despite her efforts at 'passing', Molly is really very dependent on other people. Kevin says he has to tell her everything and her sister believes she only copes at all because of the help she receives. The community nurses have had to point out that they cannot give all their time to her. Molly's reticence about openly admitting her problems only serves to compound them – as in the case of not knowing the value of money. The fear of showing herself up and her habit of jumping on anyone who draws attention to her difficulties are major hurdles in the way of improving her skills.

A capacity perspective

A closer analysis of the personal profile above shows that Molly has more about her – and more against her – than this deficiency perspective allows.

Molly's apparent shortcomings as a mother have to be seen in the context of her own upbringing and the pressures currently bearing down on her. Before setting up home with Kevin, she had had no experience of an ordinary family life nor any role models on which to base her own parenting behaviour. Abused by her father after her mother died in childbirth, she was taken into care and, after a succession of unhappy foster placements, spent most of her formative years in children's homes. She still finds it too painful to speak of her childhood.

Growing up in institutions, she never had the opportunity to acquire many domestic skills – except for some sewing and a bit of cooking she learned at a training centre. Otherwise everything was done for her. Even when she finally moved out of hostel accommodation into her own flat, just before taking up with Kevin, staff used to call in every day to keep an eye on her. The fact that shortly after, with Kevin away in London, she was managing a house and looking after a young baby on her own (while expecting a second) demonstrates both an acquired level of practical competence and her capacity for new learning.

It was during this time that she accumulated the rent arrears. The precise details are obscure. Kevin says he was sending her the rent money but the community nurse reports she was living only on her child benefit and severe disablement allowance. The £700 debt she built up over the course of this year was not the result of fecklessness or extravagance. She did not incur any debts elsewhere. Gas, electricity, coal, water rates, TV licence and rental and other regular outgoings were paid up. Rent arrears and an empty larder are pretty common symptoms among people living in poverty. Other evidence, too, shows that Molly understands the value of money even if her poor counting gives her problems handling change. For example, she knows how to use itemized receipts, and used to wash clothes by hand in the caravan to save money rather than pay at the launderette.

Molly's relationship with her children has to be seen in the light of her past. She knows she favours Tony. He reminds her of the son taken away at birth for whom she has quietly grieved ever since. This loss, and the fact that both Amy and Tony were 'under Social Services' at one time, explains much else. Apart from undermining her self-esteem and sense of worth as a mother, she feels under constant pressure to prove herself to others. She also feels that any mistake she makes may result in her losing the children. She dare not admit to her difficulties, strenuously denying them for fear of the consequences.

The charge that Molly puts her own wants and needs before those of her children is not borne out by the facts. Indeed, she agreed to have Kevin's baby against her own instincts. On the occasions she has left home, only the children have brought her back. And now, against the dictates of her own heart, she has agreed to sign them over to Kevin so they can have a proper home.

Molly does her best for the children against the odds. Keeping them looking clean on the caravan site is an impossible task when the only space they have for play is outside. In any case, Amy and Tony look no worse than neighbouring children. Mud and dirt are constantly being trailed into the caravan. Hand-washing clothes is not enough to stop them becoming grubby. In such conditions, cleanliness is a losing battle. When she was given an old twin-tub Molly quickly set to work washing everything she could lay her hands on.

Like many new mothers, Molly needed a lot of help with her first child. From Kevin's account of her emotional state at this time it seems possible she was suffering from postnatal depression. She had no family to turn to and naturally looked to Kevin. Just at this point he went off to work in London. By the time Tony came along she had learned to cope and had acquired good-enough child care skills to avoid the sort of problems she had encountered with Amy. She shows a proper concern for the children's safety and well-being. She is aware of the danger presented by the gas cooker; leaves the caravan door open regardless of the cold so she can keep an eye on the children playing outside; and moves the children out of their damp bedroom in winter.

Molly lacks motivation rather than skills. Again this can be seen as a response to her circumstances. She hates living in the caravan and the strain has brought her down. Certainly her behaviour shows signs of the traumatic effects of stress including decreased functioning, withdrawal, anger and fear. Much of her apparent apathy is probably the result of depression. Television provides a means of escape from the daily grind of a life cramped by poverty. It is notable that when Molly's black moods lift for a spell she sets to work with gusto.

Molly is the victim of gendered assumptions by Kevin and by service workers that unjustly show her up in a bad light. It was Kevin who went to London, returning home for a week only once every three months, yet Molly who is blamed for the problems that ensued. Kevin is critical of her for not using contraceptives, when she says she couldn't cope with another child, while failing to take precautions himself on the grounds that he's 'not bothered'. Even though Kevin questions Molly's understanding of the value of money he still leaves her to do the shopping on her own. Likewise, although Kevin is now off work, he still expects Molly to walk the 40-minute round trip to school three times a day to deliver and collect the children. As evidence of her apathy he cites her refusal to break off watching TV to make him a cup of tea, obliging him to get up and do it for himself. Molly herself was angered by the fact that, while she had been expected to cope with both children at home in the caravan all day, the community nurses had provided Kevin with day care for two days a week when she left him. In this context, some of Molly's alleged failings are more properly seen as a function of other people's, especially Kevin's, views of her role as a (common-law) wife and mother.

Molly has received little parenting support from the health and welfare services. Service delivery tends to be crisis-orientated: Molly has been left to cope as best she can until things go wrong. Her past experience has taught her to be wary of social workers who, in any case, tend to move on so frequently as to prevent the formation of trusting relationships. The community nurses have provided valuable practical and emotional support but often too little and too late. For example, efforts were made to help Molly with her reading but the support was not sustained until she had the confidence to go alone. There is a tendency for these shortcomings in the services to be personalized and the blame pinned on Molly. It is not so much that she has failed as that she has not been given a chance to succeed.

Conclusions

A 'deficiency orientation' underpins the presumption of incompetence that fosters an expectation of parenting failure among practitioners. It also encourages the mistake of seeing parents' problems entirely in terms of their own limitations, so blaming the victims for difficulties that owe more to the pressures in their lives and the constraints of their situation. In terms of professional practice and service delivery, this approach exhibits a number of characteristic features. Assessment and review tend to lay stress on finding out what people cannot do, and to define them in terms of their deficiencies and failings. Planning is primarily resource-led, with people being fitted into existing services rather than services being designed to fit their needs. Case management relies on professional judgement and decision-making and allows little scope for user choice and participation.

Molly Austin's story shows how such attitudes and practices may originate, how they are sustained, and how they may be overcome in order to pave the way for a more positive approach. Practitioners or researchers who adopt a 'deficiency perspective' are led ineluctably into attributing Molly's plight and her problems to her own limitations and lack of competence. In contrast, by acknowledging her skills and the impact of environmental and social pressures on her ability to cope, a 'capacity perspective' reveals new options for practical help and support.

Research has shown (see Chapter 2) that the attitude of people providing support for parents with learning difficulties is one of the key factors determining its success. A 'deficiency orientation' relegates people to a dependent status as passive recipients of services. A 'capacity perspective' would recognize Molly's resourcefulness and seek ways for her to deal with her rent arrears. Her problems are not the result of lack of competence but stem primarily from lack of money. Dealing with Molly's debts would offer her choices and enable her to reassert control over her life. It would also allow the family to remain together. Families can be set up to fail or helped to overcome. The opportunity to help Molly Austin is still there. Otherwise she is destined to remain on the caravan site, alone.

CHAPTER 7

Knowing Rosie Spencer: the story of a research relationship

She is standing at the window of her small terraced house as I park outside. Coming out to greet me, she smiles. It is her birthday. Inside, family and friends are gathered and, after finding me a chair, she places it close to hers. Her daughter, Beth, sits the other side of me. Wedding photographs of her younger son, Paul, are pulled out of a drawer and she names all the beaming faces. On the wall hang pictures of her two grandchildren, Guy and Cathy. All around the room, greetings cards and presents jostle for space with ornaments, family photos and mementoes. We talk awhile. Later she introduces me to Sally, her daughter-in-law, and then her husband, Charlie. He shakes my hand warmly. The women sit together in the living room and the men crowd noisily into the kitchen. In between, on a cloth covered table, lies the birthday feast. This was our beginning.

A week later, in early August, I phone Rosie. Her first question is when will I be going to see her again, her second is do I like her. We arrange an afternoon later in the week.

Rosie is again waiting at the window for me to arrive. Charlie has gone out. We sit around the fire and talk for a couple of hours.

'I keep falling, everything's going black at front of me. Community nurse thinks I'm making it up, falling down on purpose. I keep feeling sick all time. I've got pains in my stomach. I've got high blood pressure an' all. They don't know what's wrong with me yet, I'm waiting for my blood test coming. I went last time and it weren't back. Community nurse meets me in town, can't go on my own, I get played 'ummer with. Because I were going every week and she said that's too much. They shout at me, community nurses do. I take no notice of them. Doctor wanted to see me every month and Community Nurse Sharpe says, I think it's six weeks she should go. I don't like her, she's too bossy. I have a lady doctor, Dr Ellis, she's nice. I can go in by myself and see her if I wish, but I let Community Nurse Brightside come in.

She says, if you show me up I'll walk out. But I haven't done, have I? I haven't done.'

'My daughter, Beth, spits in my face – it's not nice is it? – and calls me a ratbag and all stuff. It's not nice, when she's 23. You see, she's seen somebody do it in Leeds and she's copying them. I take no notice of her. Our Paul's wife pulls her up about it and our Paul says she shouldn't do that to people. But don't tell her I've told you or I'll get in trouble. Our Beth takes tablets with her having epilepsy. Our Paul used to be like that but he's grown out of them now.'

'I moved house a lot cos lads wouldn't leave me alone. Same as lads up here. I were out taking dog and them big lads says, come on Rosie, I wanna shag you, he says, get out here. So I reported it to police and they've told me if he touch me again I've got to get straight to police and they'll come. Beth and Charlie said, oh leave it – just tell your social worker. But she can't do owt can she?'

'My mother and dad's dead. I've got three brothers, I'm a twin, me. Davy lives in Bradford, I don't know whereabouts. Our Harry, he works at dustbins. I work at Salvation Army. It's my placement from Centre. I work on a Monday morning. It's all right. You don't get paid for it though.'

'I met Charlie in town, he used to sell papers. He said he wanted to go out with me. We knew each other five years before we got married. Charlie's mother didn't want him to get married. She said, "I'll buy you five suits."'

'I've three children, me. I didn't plan them, they were a surprise. After I had Beth I had my tubes tied. They wanted me to have it done. Doctor said that I didn't want any more children. He said it was better for me.'

As I leave, Rosie asks for my home telephone number.

Sunday evening, three days later, and Rosie phones. Charlie and Beth have been rowing about her new boyfriend and Rosie has felt caught in the middle. Beth, she says, has hit her across the face.

Rosie phones at the end of the same week. She says the arguments at home are making her hair fall out. She just wants me to know. Could I perhaps machine a new zip into her coat?

Sunday again and Rosie phones to say she feels dizzy after her bath and she hasn't seen her doctor yet. We agree on another meeting in five days' time.

The following Tuesday, Rosie phones to say that Community Nurse Brightside has persuaded her to postpone her doctor's appointment until after her caravan holiday in Cleethorpes. As Rosie is anxious to know the results of the tests, she is unhappy about waiting another three weeks. She is also in trouble with Charlie and Beth for agreeing to the alteration.

Friday, we meet as arranged at Rosie's house and she gives me a souvenir pen brought back from a day trip to Manchester. Charlie has phoned Community Nurse Brightside to object to the appointment being changed. The nurse has told Rosie that she was upset when Charlie shouted at her. Rosie now feels she is being blamed for the bother.

'I might not go and see community nurse this week, I'm too scared. I've got in trouble for all that and I didn't phone them, Charlie did. Never mind. I'm not saying owt else about it anyway. Community nurse is there to help you, not shout at you. They don't always. Sometimes.'

'I haven't seen my social worker for a long time. She doesn't come and see me. You've got to go there. She said she'd come to see me. She said it at my review down at Centre and she hasn't been.'

'My mother and father said they didn't like Charlie. I moved out and went to live with him in Bradford. In rooms. We was married. My social worker said I couldn't have any children. But I did.'

'We had no help when the children were small. My husband used to cope, and me. Now Beth does my ironing and shopping. I do the best I can, cleaning up. I used to work at Fox's at Batley, packed biscuits. I used to work at that home up Hull Road – make beds up and that, clean and wash up. This is when I were married. I used to work in sports centre in town, help with towels for baths and lockers. I used to get paid for that. I don't get nothing now cos I'm not working. I'd rather work at Salvation Army all time than work at Centre.'

'Charlie works in working men's club. He collects glasses. That's tonight, Saturday and Sunday. And Wednesday. But don't say I've told you, I'll get played 'ummer with. Our Paul works for railway as a guard. Our Jonathan used to work at John Cotton's but they finished him. For thumping the foreman. They had a row or something and just hit him. He used to work at supermarket but he wasn't quick enough so they finished him.'

'My doctor is Dr Lewis, my proper doctor. But I don't like seeing a man with . . . you know. I see a lady doctor. I have too many headaches, I've told her that. I nearly fell the other day. I go dizzy. I shall have some photos to show doctor when I come back from holiday.'

'Beth still loses her temper. She shouts at you and it goes through you doesn't it? Do you shout at your sons? I do tell her but she takes no notice. She sucks her thumb an' all. Well, she's 23 now. Her boyfriend says he'll break her of it.'

As I get up to leave she asks for my home address. She wants to send me a postcard from her holidays.

Sunday evening and Rosie rings in tears. She is still suffering headaches and dizzy spells and asks if I will contact her doctor. Almost at once she retracts the request, feeling she will be in trouble if I do.

The following day she phones again to say she feels even worse. I ask if she would like me to go with her to see Community Nurse Brightside tomorrow. She says yes. This time Charlie comes on the line and explains that 'Rosie gets upset about small things but the community nurse has no right to be angry with her'. He says that her concern about her test results is causing a great deal of upset and aggravation in the family. He also thinks her headaches should be investigated. It is now ten weeks since her GP took blood and urine samples and still no results have come through. Rosie is already being treated for an anxiety state and this further worry is making life unbearable for the whole family.

I collect Rosie from home and she directs me to the community health unit. We wait in reception until Community Nurse Brightside invites us into a private room and makes us all coffee. I explain that Rosie has asked me along for support: would she phone Rosie's GP to see if the results of her tests have come through yet? She does but the GP has heard nothing. I ask if she will check with the hospital. Half an hour later she finally gets hold of someone to give her the results over the phone. The nurse informs Rosie that her GP will have to discuss them with her although she does confirm that Rosie is not anaemic.

All the while we are talking, Rosie keeps glancing out at the car park and remarking that Community Nurse Sharpe's car is not there. Just as we are about to leave, she walks into the room. Whereas before Rosie had been initiating most of the conversation, she now sits, very quietly, fiddling with a bit of loose skin on her finger. Nurse Sharpe says brusquely, 'I've told you not to pick at it'. Rosie is immediately reduced to a small child and the conversation continues in the same blustering tone. Rosie cries more than once. She recounts her problems with Beth but Nurse Sharpe says she doesn't want to know about Beth and her personal affairs and that the family will have to sort it out. Nurse Sharpe points out how it was Rosie's own decision to leave the hostel and go back to Charlie and Beth two years ago. By now, Rosie is full up with tears and cannot speak. She glances out of the window again and the nurse, without pausing, snaps, 'And don't look out of the window when I'm talking to you'.

I ask why Rosie can't make an appointment with her GP when we now know she has the test results. The nurse dismisses us by saying: 'If that's what you want, it's nothing to do with me.' As we leave I realize I am feeling a little hot and dizzy myself.

Several times as we drive back to Rosie's house she says, 'You saw how she talked to me. It's not right, is it. She shouldn't talk to me like that, should she?' As she relates the morning's events to Charlie, he recalls similar conversations he has had with the same community nurse. He also adds that Rosie's nervous stress has twice caused alopecia in the past.

On the following Friday, a postcard arrives for me from Cleethorpes. It says, 'Love from Rosie, Charlie and Beth'. The next day I go on two weeks' holiday.

During the week of my return I phone Charlie and ask if I might interview him on his own. We arrange a Wednesday when Rosie is attending the Centre. He is listening to the radio when I arrive and he makes me a cup of coffee with a plate of biscuits.

'At first they didn't care for me much, her parents. We were courting for five years on and off. It were one period when we were off, you know, when we'd fallen out over a little thing, and she came to see me. She told me that she were going to have a baby. So of course I said how on earth are you going to have this baby. No, it wasn't mine. So we went into park to have a talk. We had a long talk and eventually I decided that we'd get married. My mother offered me three suits a year not to get married. But when we did, my mother thought the world of her, Rosie couldn't do a wrong thing.'

'Social Services wanted to take the child straight off her without her seeing the child. These doctors came to my works before I got married. They said to me, you shouldn't get married to her, like, because you'll have nothing but trouble. So I says, well, what's happening to the child? So they told me that they'd take her in a home, let her have this child, and take it direct away from her. So I says, don't you think that's a bit harsh? I says, what if somebody came to your place of employment and said these things to you. I said, are you married and have you got children? I says, did anyone come to your employment saying that they're taking your fiancée away from you and having the child took into care? What are you trying to make out she is? Even animals has their own young, I says, but you're making out that she couldn't look after the child. I says, and what on earth am I? I may be disabled, I says, but I've got two hands, I've got two legs, and my fiancée has two hands and two legs. I says, she's a human being. I says, I disagree with you.'

'She went in hospital to have the baby and I made all the arrangements to pick her up. So her mother interfered. She collected her. They says Rosie can't look after it. I says, what's wrong with me? 'Oh, you can't look after it.' I says to Rosie, your parents are not going to look after it. If we can't look after him after all I've done, I says, no one is. So I says the best thing to do is, we'll go and see your social worker and have the child put in care.'

'I could see that she were getting very, very upset because they wouldn't even let her touch the child, and it were same with me. I says to her social worker, I think to settle Rosie it'd be best if you took the child away into a children's home. I says, we've spoken about it and that is our decision. I says, we think her parents shouldn't have the authority over us. After all, I says, I gave the child my name. I'm asking you to take the child in care so Rosie can get back and be happy again.'

'At first the social worker says, well, I think the child would be all right with her parents. I says, but I don't. I'm asking you to take the child in care. I says, if you don't I'll see somebody further. So she says, you can't. I says, are you trying to tell me that you've got the full authority over me and Rosie? If you refuse, I'll go higher than you. I says, I want the child taking away into care and then me and my wife can go and see the child, and have the advantage of picking the child up, so she feels like a mother and I feel like a father, instead of going and just looking at the child. So that's what happened.'

'Jonathan went into care when he were a month old. First he was in a nursery and then he went into a children's home. We tried to apply to have him back – I think he would be about one. They didn't feel it would be right. So from there we didn't ask no more until he were six. We got him back but it didn't work out. He were getting very upset, he just couldn't fit in home life. They agreed to take him back. He were there all his life up to him being 18. Then he lived on his own until he got marrried. I think he were 21 to 22 year old. He's getting divorced now.'

'Jonathan keeps himself to himself, he doesn't bother over us at all. Mind you, it's more or less mutual. I put it this way, if he doesn't want to bother with us, it's all right with me. If he comes he gets treated all right, we talk to him all right. We buy grandchildren presents. We don't see them very often.'

'It were seven years after Jonathan we had Paul and Beth. There were no question of them going into care when they were born. They brought Paul from Marylands, where he were born, direct home and they must have tried to show her how to care for him, how to put nappies on or something like that. The point is they didn't show me. No one were there to help me, you see. When she came home with him he were put into my hands, and no one ever came and told me how to make a bottle or anything. So what I had to do, I had to take notice of how I took the nappy off, I had to ask how to make a baby's bottle. So everything were all right. I managed. We were supposed to have a nurse come and advise us. Only time she saw the children is when we took them up to the clinic for weighing. We both took them. But I were the one that undressed them and put them on the scales. In fact, she once asked me how I kept my nappies like they was. I kept them white, you know.'

'No, Rosie didn't breastfeed, they had to pump her out. The point was that she were terrified of touching them. They were too small. She were frightened in dropping them or something like that or injuring them in any way. That's more or less why I had to take over when they come home, you see. They were one year old and then she would pick them up.'

'Until they were about two year old I had to stop work, then I started working again. But neither of them were left alone with Rosie. I took a night job; they were 12-hour shifts what I were doing an' all. I made it so I could be home when they were up. I were at work when they were asleep. That's the way I had to make it you see, even when they were little. The only trouble was, I were only having three hours' sleep.'

'Only time she couldn't manage with the children, it were for bathing or giving them food or anything. She couldn't feed them or anything. She couldn't even change a nappy. Everything what had to be done for them, I had to do it. But as far as looking after them, if there weren't anything to do for them she could manage. I started work at seven o'clock at night, I got home for about seven o'clock, had a sleep on settee from seven o'clock till nine. As soon as I heard them waking, the children, I woke up myself, you see, so I could attend to their needs. What I did, they were first on ordinary nappies and it were when these disposal nappies came out, I decided to put them into them. So I shown Rosie how to put them on, and I let her do that.'

'No social workers bothered us. I would have liked a bit of help when I come home from work, I could have done with about two to three hours. So I could have had a bit extra sleep like, you know. What happened, I had a breakdown at that time. With working 12-hour shifts and having three hours' sleep, this was every day, you know, I broke down. I got a very big migraine. I kept having headaches and my eyes were fading, going dizzy and that. They sent me to Pinderfields Hospital and I had a brain scan and the doctor said I had to stop working. If I hadn't stopped working I would have been dead. It were exhaustion.'

'At that particular time it didn't bother me a bit over going out, I didn't want to go out. I just wanted to be at home with my family to give them the care I felt what were needed for them. I never bothered anyone, I were very – what do you call it? – independent. I were too independent to ask for owt. I wouldn't say my neighbours wouldn't have helped me if I asked them, but I didn't bother.'

'My mother didn't give us any support with the children, she wasn't able to. The point is I never asked, which I think I should have done. I think I would have got the help. I mean, I've three sisters. You see, I never went looking for it. I were trying to prove my point of what I said to the three doctors. They were all against us having these children, you see. I had to prove it can be done.'

'When Paul were ten and Beth were nine, they decided – after all bedwetting and things like that and we were clear from that – they decided to take them into care. They did try to accuse me of hitting them with a dog chain, which I never did. But, you see, I couldn't prove it.'

'It were when I were after a gas cooker, you see, because gas cooker broke. So of course I took them all down – Rosie, two children and lot – and they says, can we have a word with children on their own? I says, what for? They says, oh, we just want to see how they are. So after that she says, don't take these children out of here. I says, what on earth's up? She says, well, Paul has told me you've been hitting him with a dog chain. I says, I beg your pardon, I says, I would never do that to my children. I says, I've cared for them all this time, I've given them what love I could ever give them, and do you think I'm going to hit my children with a chain? I says I may have tapped them on their knee, on their leg, I says, but I've never hit them. So they says, oh well, you can't take them out. Paul were 14 when he come out of care, and Beth were 15 when I got her home.'

'I couldn't tell you if a doctor looked at them. They wouldn't tell me nothing. And it were only me going down for cooker. We had access, we could go and see the children every week.'

'What led up to Paul coming out at 14, you see, I'd been forward and back to court about three to four times trying to get them back home. They were supposed to be in care until they were 18, that's what I were given to understand by the court. So what happened after that, you see, I changed my solicitor and the one I changed to weren't working for Social Services. They were having a bit of trouble with Paul with fires or something. Paul wouldn't settle where Beth was. He had a grievance with them, you see, so they moved him. He were setting fires and all sorts. So they sent him home to me to put up with it. I just talked to him like what I could do. I mean, I'll admit, I were very strict with him when he come home at 14, I were very strict. He didn't rather like it but that wasn't the point. He did as he were told. I didn't have to use anything on him, didn't have to smack him or owt like that. When I said a thing, he knew.'

'He settled down until he were 17 and then he just wanted to go. So he went into a place bed and breakfast, and then he got a flat and he started courting. Rosie were away for two years, you see, at Lee Bank Hostel and we were across with one another, so I were going to get a divorce because she didn't seem to want to come home again with me.'

'When Paul got to know that I'd put in for this divorce, he came into club. He hit me on top of head with a glass of shandy, pint. I don't know how glass didn't go into my head, it broke, and when I come home, house were on fire. Well, it had been, it were smoking and all that. He went to court for it. He got two to three months. And it's altered him. Oh, it brought him round. He's one of grandest lads going now, he can't do enough for me now sort of thing.'

'When Beth came home she were all right, but I had a few problems with school. They were upsetting her at school and one thing and another. And of course Beth, she gets annoyed, she's the same temperament as her mother. They argue pretty frequently. I'm generally the one in middle, separating them. Rosie can be a terror. If she's really annoyed, anything Rosie has in her hand it will go, she'll throw it at you. So you see, it's been a problem all my married life I've had with her.'

'We've lived all over since we were married. First, my sister had a flat what I had at Bradford. From there we went to Carlton, Dobroyd, again back to Carlton, to Potters Crescent, to Wentworth, Neets Crescent, and then here. Rosie couldn't settle. You see, if local children says anything to her, well, she'll take it deeply to heart and she seems to get right upset. I mean we've even had it here but what I've done, you see, I found out where the children's lived and I've gone to see the parents myself. They just calling her names, you know. That's one thing she won't take, things like that. And, of course, Rosie's retaliated, you see, and played pop with them, and, of course, they're going to do it all the more. That's reason why we've had to keep moving you see, to get into a place where nobody knows her. But the point is, when they do get to know her, it only comes again and then I have to go see a psychiatrist to ask for a letter stating that through reason of being upset we'll have to move. We've had to have a priority every time for house.'

'You see, Rosie is a very nervous person. She were away four and a half years at Hester Hall Annexe. Four and a half years for hitting a fella on top of head with a bicycle lamp. We were having an argument, you see, and this friend of mine came and tried to grab hold of her. He came in interfering. Well, I tried to ask him to leave it but he took no notice. He grabbed her by the arm, and of course she turned round – and we kept this bicycle lamp on top of telly – she picked it up and hit him with it. He had to have twelve stitches, so they'd to go to court. The Annexe? It was psychiatric. Jonathan were born then but he wasn't with us. That's why it went to seven years before the next one came, because she were four and a half years away. They sent me, like, a little file, from psychiatrists – a solicitor's got it now – and what it said that Rosie was severe subnormal, a mind of a child at seven, and she would never alter. I seem to agree with the doctors in that one respect but, oh, she alters. She's altered a good deal in past. But I wish I knew what gets her cross.'

'You see, she's different with someone in authority. Me or Beth, we're not authority, you see, we just live in the same household, sort of thing. It's when she gets up she's either feeling sick or she's headache or one thing and another, and at times it does irritate. It causes a good bit of friction with Beth, I mean she gets upset a bit does Beth over it.'

'The reason she went into the hostel was she had a type of breakdown, she couldn't get on with either of us, me or Beth. She were throwing pots at us, she were throwing boiling tea at us. We used to walk out. Well, she used to lock the door. We used to have to stop out until she decided we could come in. She were at the hostel for two years, I think. It were decided I'd try and see if she'd come back into living within a family unit again, you see. She were coming home for weekends. At first there were no way and then gradually it were getting better and better.'

'You see, I don't sleep with Rosie. Since Paul and Beth were born, about two to three years after, I decided to let her sleep on her own. At first, when she come home from the hostel, she was sleeping with Beth in Beth's bedroom. Well, it were causing arguments. I made out that my legs were getting worse, and I couldn't walk up steps all time, so I asked Beth if she want me to bring my bed down, which she did. I says to Beth, now you have your own bedroom, mother has her own and I've mine. Rosie were very happy about it.'

'Only contraception before then, if I did use contraception, it were me with the sheath. She's had the coil. But she couldn't get on with it. She had a lot of bleeding. She couldn't walk because as she were walking it were just like a tap. I took her straight to hospital myself. I told them what were happening, so they told me what it more or less was. I says right, have it out. 'Oh we can't do that, she can't have no sex or anything because she might get pregnant again.' I said I'm not entirely bothered, I said, but take the bloody thing out. I says don't worry, there won't be no more.'

'I've had to fight, in fact biggest part of my married life I've had to fight for Rosie and I've also had to fight for the children. I've never had a smooth run sort of thing. I hardly get any affection back from her. If anyone caused me any harm or anything, she'd be the first one to stand up against them. Rosie isn't a type of person what will show you what you've done for her or anything like that, but you see she's good. She's a lovable woman, she's a person you could love. Well, I have done up to thirty-odd years like. I mean, the point is with Rosie, you've got to show her the respect. You can do things for her which she can't thank you for or anything like that. That's what upsets Beth, like if she does her ironing for her and Rosie won't say thank you. But she shows it in other things. I mean to be truthful, she's a good person. I said I were getting married not for love, for spite. I wanted to prove a point. They didn't think Rosie were fit to get married. We've been married for, I think it's 34 years now. Out of that she's been away about six and a half years. I mean, no one can tell me that a person like Rosie isn't the marrying type because a person like Rosie is. They may not show it in the way they speak to you or what they do, it's other ways. You've to live with a person before you can experience it. It were a couple of years before it grew, before I did really love her. That's what I found. It's a very funny thing, with a person like Rosie, to say you really love her but you do, you do get to love a person like Rosie.'

After the weekend I phone Rosie and arrange to see her on Thursday afternoon. She tells me she has run out of tablets and also needs to see the optician. I ask her if she sees me as a kind of community nurse. She says no, a friend.

Thursday, and both Rosie and Charlie are waiting for me. She has bought me a present from her holiday – a pot bell in the shape of a woman wearing a long skirt. Charlie makes us all a cup of coffee and we sit down.

'Been to Centre yesterday. I work in kitchen, I were on salad bar. I have to serve it, because cooks what prepare it. Sort Christmas cards out. They tell me to sort cards out and then, before I come home, I help them to pile all chairs and fold table covers up, and we wash some cupboards out and put everything back, hang table covers out, take them out of drier, polish silver up, wash bottle tops and dries them. We have us dinner at half past 11, them who's in kitchen. That's early, isn't it?'

'I've to go to court on Thursday. For not pay my poll tax. Charlie hasn't paid his, he can't on his money. (Rosie shows me her court summons although she cannot read it. She owes £93.83 plus £12 summons costs.) Anybody can't pay that.'

'I haven't told community nurse because it's nowt to do with her really. I showed social worker and she made me look at it outside. She talks to me in passageway. She says show me it and she said, "I can't help you". She said she can't do owt for me because it's too late.'

'Look, have you seen my toe? Look. I must have banged it on holiday. If community nurse can't take me to doctor I'll go on my own, I've told her. She won't let me. Charlie?'

'Look, Rosie, all you have to do is make an appointment and keep it to yourself. You see, what you do, Rosie, you're there ringing her telling her every little thing you do, so you're giving her things to pick you up on. There's things what you should keep to yourself. All you need to say to her, "Is it possible for you to get me someone what'll understand me better?" To me, she's treating Rosie as a child, that's how I see it. You see, when you're in the hostel, Rosie, you've to go by their rules. Now you're at home, you go by your own rules. What you don't want to tell her you don't and then she can't pull you up on it. That's what I've been trying to advise her. With Rosie keep going to her telling her these things, it's making community nurse as though she's the gaffer, sort of thing, that's over her. If Rosie didn't tell her these things, she couldn't say no.'

'Yes, but she shouts, that isn't helping. She shouts at me. I told Nurse Sharpe last week I wanted somebody else. She won't let me speak. She's to have all say, hasn't she? She's having a baby January. That's near Christmas, isn't it?'

As I leave, Charlie thanks me for coming and says I can call at any time. He insists that in future I just walk in the door rather than knock. Rosie is off to buy some fish and chips and I give her a lift. A group of young lads watch her as she walks into the shop.

Sunday evening Rosie phones to say she has an appointment with her doctor about her swollen leg. Will I go with her? I cannot. Will I then go with her to court this next Thursday about her poll tax? I agree to meet her and Charlie outside the magistrates court. She tells me she has been to the community health unit to see about changing her community nurse. The receptionist had told her she couldn't.

Three days later Charlie phones to say he is glad I am going with them tomorrow. I explain about the poll tax exemption for people with 'severe mental impairment'. Does he think she might feel insulted if a claim is made on these grounds? Charlie says that Rosie will not understand what we are talking about. He is willing to give it a try.

It is a gloomy October day. Rosie and Charlie are waiting for me outside the court. After a brief discussion with Rosie about exemption we arrange to see a counsellor. Consultation takes place in the public entrance hall alongside others on the same business. The counsellor asks to see Rosie's invalidity pension book and we are told her GP must sign a form. As neither Charlie nor Rosie can read, they ask for any forms be sent to me for forwarding to Rosie's GP. In all this time the counsellor addresses herself exclusively to me, as if Rosie and Charlie are invisible.

Afterwards we go for a cup of coffee in the bus station café. I am feeling uneasy about labelling Rosie but she and Charlie are more than pleased to be relieved of the debt. A couple of days later I receive the forms and send them to Rosie's GP.

A week passes and then Rosie phones on the Saturday. We arrange for me to visit her early in the week to see what she does at the Salvation Army hall.

Rosie greets me as I walk into the hall. Her colleagues are expecting me, too. The women are very friendly and Rosie is treated as one of the team. Just as I am beginning to think that community placements are good for integration, an older woman puts her arms around the shoulders of Rosie and a young man and says, 'You're my children today aren't you?' Rosie, a grandmother, mutters 'Children!' under her breath.

The following Thursday Charlie phones to say they have received a means-test form for the community charge. Beth is refusing to explain it to them so I agree to call in next week.

Tuesday, and the door to their house opens as I arrive. After reading the form out to them I phone the community charge officer who explains it is a formality to establish the best way for them to pay. I point out that a claim for exemption is pending, but the officer warns that if the form is not returned within 14 days Rosie will be liable for a £400 fine. We complete and post the form. I arrange with Rosie to call in and see her at the Centre on Wednesday week.

The Centre manager introduces me to Rosie's keyworker. Just then Rosie comes through the door. I can see she has been crying. She has a cold and won't be allowed to help in the kitchens today. Instead she will be cleaning brasses.

Inside the workroom two groups of people are sat at tables with staff. Some are washing and drying silver paper while others polish brass and copperware donated to the Centre for selling at their coffee mornings. For a small charge, the public can bring in items for cleaning. Staff have also arranged for 'students' to do ironing for homeless people. The money raised is donated to charity. There is little conversation and, during the hour or so I sit there, Rosie cleans one brass kettle. She says she wants to leave the Centre and find a job.

At noon we queue up for lunch. Rosie chooses a hot meal – pork, roast potatoes, cabbage and gravy followed by steamed pudding. Community Nurse Sharpe makes a fleeting appearance. Rosie spots her but she ignores us. After lunch we sit and talk in the social room. Rosie outlines her weekly routine. On Mondays she helps at the Salvation Army hall in the morning, returning to the Centre for the afternoon; Tuesdays she is at home but usually pays her community nurse a visit; Wednesdays she attends the Centre all day; Thursday mornings she helps at the hall again; Fridays she is at home or visits her friends; Saturdays she sees her son, Paul; and Sundays she goes to church.

She tells me of her recent visit to her GP. Her blood tests are clear and the doctor thinks the blackouts may be caused by her tablets. Rosie had explained the difficulties she is having with Beth but the GP only asked if she wanted to return to the hostel she had lived in two years ago.

It is now December and over two weeks pass before Rosie phones again to say she has crushed her finger in the door and her nose keeps bleeding. She is off to the doctor's tomorrow. She has been chased by some young lads when walking home from the bus. Community Nurse Sharpe has left and Rosie has given her a soft toy for her new baby.

Four days later Rosie phones with the news that Beth has taken an overdose and is in the psychiatric unit. She asks if I will give her a lift to the hospital on Thursday, but unfortunately I have another appointment. The next day I phone to ask about Beth, and Charlie tells me how she has been suffering from bouts of depression since being raped four years ago. He says she needs a woman to talk to about it. I agree to visit her with them.

Early next morning Charlie phones. Rosie has received a community charge demand for £487.65. It is now two months since I posted the claim for exemption to Rosie's GP. Further enquiries reveal that exemption has been granted but has not yet been entered on the computer. The balance is nil. Charlie is relieved. He has other good news. His application for mobility allowance has been granted ('I'm a spastic. I've been like that all my life. Now I'm getting a lot of pain in my legs').

The following Wednesday I phone to check that Beth is still in hospital. Charlie informs me that she has overdosed again. She had been out and bought some aspirins at the local shop. I arrange a time to pick them up.

Rosie has not returned from the Salvation Army hall when I arrive. Charlie warns me that she is unaware of the second overdose. They have visited Beth nearly every day but no one has explained anything to them. I suggest that Charlie makes the first move by asking for an appointment with the consultant. I enquire if they are coping without her and learn that he is paying a friend £2 to do the ironing while she is in hospital. Rosie arrives home apologetic. She has been buying some fruit and cigarettes for Beth.

We meet Beth on the ward. There is no outward display of affection, they just say hello. Beth wants us to go to the hospital café for a drink and we walk there in a straggled line. Sitting in the café, Rosie relays the current news but Beth only wants to know if her dog misses her. Charlie says he is going to ask if she can come out for Christmas, but Beth wants to stay in hospital until she is sorted out. She tells her parents she doesn't want them to visit every day, only every other day. Looking at Beth's exposed arms it is evident that she has started to mutilate herself. She tells us she has done it with drawing pins from the notice board.

At some point Beth and I are left on our own while Charlie and Rosie go to see about an appointment with the consultant. I put my arm around Beth's shoulders to comfort her and she hugs me. She says she can't talk about what's upsetting her, neither can she talk to her mum and dad about it. 'I know my mum can't help it because she was born like that but I need someone to talk to.' She still feels like committing suicide and has done for some time. She is sad that her boyfriend cannot understand why she has done it. He thinks she is 'nutty'. She asks if I will visit her again. I say yes. (My subsequent visits to Beth Spencer, our friendship and what we spoke about over a number of months remain confidential.)

Rosie and Charlie return and say goodbye to Beth. Charlie tells Beth to hug her mother which she does. Charlie just walks out.

Christmas and all is quiet.

The first day back at work after New Year and Rosie phones to ask when I am going to see her again. We arrange next Wednesday evening. On Sunday, she phones because her thumb is bleeding. She is alone in the house.

Rosie is standing at the window peering out into the darkness. She greets me at the door. Charlie's father had died in the early hours of the morning. After asking me to rebandage her thumb, which is still bleeding, she shows me her Christmas presents.

'Have you seen my new skirt and my new jumper? Our Beth bought me that Foster and Allen tape. Our Paul and Sally bought me that – Harry Secombe. Look, had them bought as well, cushion covers. I bought Charlie that video. Charlie bought me that handbag on chair, there.'

'We're going on holiday in July anyway. Sally's going with us this year, and her mother. Paul'd be working, he works on trains. I were upset about Charlie's dad when I got to know. Community Nurse Sharpe's had a baby. What if she shouts at baby then, poor little thing? She's bringing it to see me.'

'Beth's boyfriend's mad about her taking tablets. What if I took some tablets then? I told Dr Ellis I don't want to stay here. I can't go to shop. Group of them, they're calling me all time when I'm not saying owt to them. When I were folding washing up tonight a lad nearly come in our house. They call him Chuck. He said get over there, I'll smack you one. I said you hit me you'll get it back. Charlie's been to see his father and his father says he's to leave me alone. I mean I've got to walk down road, haven't I? They say all sorts but I take no notice of them. But it's not right, is it? Police said they can't do owt until they hurt me. But it might be too late then, might it? Once, that Chuck waited for me getting off of bus. I run up road, but you shouldn't have to do that.'

'Jonathan's living in Leeds in hostel. He doesn't come up here. I get on with Jonathan all right but he's never lived with us. We used to visit him in children's home. We used to go every week. He doesn't want a divorce from his wife – it's not up to him really, is it? They were always rowing you see. It's no good for children that, is it?'

Sunday evening again and Rosie phones to say she had taken an overdose of tablets last Wednesday. I am perplexed as I had visited her the same evening and she had seemed her usual self. She tells me she had felt upset by three youths harassing her on her way home. Rosie's doctor has told the community nurses to contact the police and local headmaster. All Rosie's tablets have been removed from the house and she is being given them daily at the surgery. Beth has been discharged from hospital.

Rosie phones the next day. She has seen her doctor and told her she wants to leave home. She says she will take more tablets. Charlie has a word with me and says he is very depressed by it all. He feels she must go her own way. I arrange to see them the next evening.

Rosie, Charlie and Beth are all watching television. Beth's social worker is coming to see them on Thursday to discuss the prospect of her moving into a flat of her own. He has informed Beth that he will be bringing a student with him. Everyone is annoyed by this as he hasn't checked with them to see if they agree.

The following Sunday Rosie phones. She is still wanting to move into her own place. Charlie has said that if she does, and Beth moves out also, then he might consider seeking a one-bedroom bungalow for himself. I learn that Rosie and Beth take a cooked meal on Sundays to an old lady who lives nearby. We arrange a meeting on Friday.

When I arrive Rosie is sitting quietly on her own.

'Charlie and Beth were worried about me, they've been up to Unit, you see, and they thought I'd took some more tablets. I says I haven't. I haven't took any, I've only took my own.'

'I'm going away for two weeks to think things over. They're finding me somewhere. I tell you, there's a lot of rows in here and it's me what's causing it. Well, our Beth's always saying, "Come on, you bag, get in here", and I don't like that what she talks to me. I've even had rows with Charlie, you see. We row about all sorts, and doctor said I've to go in my bedroom and count ten. I said I'd like to go back to hostel, and unit manager said they're full up. There's a waiting list to go in there. I want to go somewhere for two week. To think it over.'

It is now the beginning of February. I phone Rosie but she has gone out. Charlie tells me he now has a psychiatric nurse calling as he feels to be under a lot of stress with Rosie and Beth. He has headaches and has become short tempered. He feels he is having to be both mother and father to Beth. Rosie has an appointment to see a consultant psychiatrist next Tuesday.

Sunday evening and Rosie phones. Beth has overdosed again. Rosie cannot understand why she keeps doing it. The following day Rosie phones to tell me she has been very upset and has cried all night.

Late the next evening Rosie phones and says she's overdosed. She doesn't know what the tablets are called or how many she has taken. She can't remember the size or colour. She asks me not to tell the community nurse or 'she'll play 'ummer'. Charlie is at home and tells me he thinks she has taken about six paracetamol. He is not going to do anything about it. Rosie says she has been upset by her visit to the psychiatrist when she felt she was being blamed for the domestic upheavals. After seeking Charlie's reassurance that Rosie is in no danger I arrange to see her tomorrow at the Centre.

Rosie tells me of her interview with the psychiatrist. She hadn't liked his questions and had left in tears. He asked how much Charlie drinks and smokes, was the house clean, had she ever been in a police cell, and why didn't she save up and take herself on a two-week holiday. He told her that she was tense and needed stronger tranquillizers. Another appointment has been fixed in two weeks – this time with Charlie and Beth.

Rosie phones on the Sunday but I am out. The next day I return her call. She has just heard that she is to be admitted tomorrow to a hostel for people with learning difficulties. She says I can visit her there at 2.00 p.m. I ask if she's happy about going and she tells me it's only for two weeks. She will continue to attend the Centre and the Salvation Army.

At the hostel, Rosie shows me her bedroom and I ask what had happened yesterday.

'Community Nurse Brightside were at home when I came home. She says, can I see you on your own in your bedroom? I said yes. She just told me I were going in hostel tomorrow. I were shocked. I were only told last Tuesday I couldn't come in. I said, are you joking? She said no. Well, Charlie said, it's quick, isn't it, that. Our Beth says, it's nowt to do with me. Community Nurse Brightside says it is, it's your mother after all. I've got my own life to live, Beth said. But she were a bit upset when I went, you know, when I went in car this morning. I didn't feel ready. They didn't tell me, you see. But I still felt like going because our Beth, she were rowing this morning.'

'Packed last night. Charlie said nowt much. Our Beth's coming to see me Thursday night. He didn't say when he was coming to see me. I want him to come and see me. Charlie's birthday, it were, on Saturday what's gone. I bought him a lighter, me.'

'I took Charlie's, you know, them heart tablets he has for his heart? I took paracetamol as well. And doctor asked me why I took them so I told her because of what psychiatrist said to me. Good job Community Nurse Sharpe wasn't there, "Stop looking out of window," she'd have said. I haven't seen baby yet, everybody's seen it except me.'

'At church, they prayed for me Sunday. Because I got upset. I started crying. I got upset and they prayed for me.'

'Last time it were a different reason why I came in hostel. They locked me out and I said I'd got bruises, I'd got all bruises all over me. Charlie said he didn't touch me so they locked me outside and I couldn't get back in. Doctors says somebody hit me one. They said it were Charlie who knocked me. I used to argue because I only had £5. I hit Charlie and then he hit me back.'

'Community nurse's coming here for me Thursday. Doctor's. She's going to ask her to put me on a stronger tablet when I'm in here. To calm me down, she said. I didn't ask to come in here, I asked to go somewhere else – you know what I mean? But that's only place I could come. But I know staff here, you see. I've got my own bedroom anyway.'

'Officer in charge were on when I came here. She said pleased to have you back, you'll be able to help me.'

Rosie walks to the car park and waves me goodbye. I arrange to see her in a week's time to see how she's settled.

Saturday, and Rosie phones me from the club to say she will be out on Tuesday with Beth who is going to look at a homeless persons' hostel. We arrange for me to call round on Monday evening.

'Beth came on Thursday. But Charlie hasn't been to see me. He said he'd come. But he were mad about our Beth getting this hostel thing Thursday, you see. They weren't speaking. Well, they weren't Saturday when I went in club. But I only stayed while about ten o'clock with being in hostel, you see.'

'I don't know many people here. I did my washing last night, right, and put two lots in drier, and then I washed, I dried up and then I put my clean sheets on bed, I had a bath and went downstairs for my tablets, stopped down there a bit and then I went to bed. It was after half past ten because I'd to wait for people coming out of bath, you see, before I could have one. It's awkward here, you know what I mean. I go home next Tuesday. I don't know if I'm looking forward to it.'

'I've to think it over, community nurse said. They're always rowing all time – it's no good me going home, is it? Do you think with high blood pressure you get a lot of headaches? That's what doctor said. She said it's with my blood pressure and she changed my tablets. I felt all right and now this morning they said, what they done to you, you looked as if you've been doped, staff said. I'm on red sleeping tablets at night and these three times a day now. Get some sheets, she says, take washing out for me, fold table covers up. Staff!'

'It's nearly done, isn't it? I'm on my last week now. Do you know how much I've to pay to stop in here? £36.50 out of my pension! Community Nurse Brightside says if you're upset come and see me, you can ring and come and see me at unit. But if Community Nurse Sharpe is there I won't go. That doctor came to see me on Thursday for that thing what Charlie's getting. Invalidity. He had me walking outside and took my blood pressure. I said, what happens now. He said go ask them in office. It's nowt to do with these in office, has it?'

Two days later Beth phones to say her mum is upset because her dad doesn't visit. Beth has tried to explain it is because he dislikes the hostel.

I phone Rosie at the hostel next day and she tells me she has decided not to go home yet because of all the arguments. Beth has been down to the Salvation Army hall to see her and shouted at her. Charlie hasn't visited.

Six days later I phone Rosie's house at tea time expecting her to have returned home but no one answers. I find that she is still at the hostel. A review had been held that afternoon to discuss her future. Rosie's family had not been invited. It had been agreed that Rosie should remain at the hostel, move into a hostel flat and eventually out into a community home when one becomes available.

The next day Charlie phones to talk about Rosie's decision. He cannot understand why she has not chosen to come home. He believes she has already become institutionalized. No one had phoned him or Beth after the review to tell them of the outcome, and in the end Beth had phoned the hostel later in the evening to find out what was happening.

The following Tuesday I visit Rosie in her new flat at the hostel which she shares with another woman, Alice. The flat consists of a large living room, two bedrooms, kitchen, WC, bathroom and spare room.

'I can't have my doctor when I live here. I've to go to one in town. I'm upset. Never mind. I don't get on with my flatmate so well. She's always telling me to go out of here all time. She's always talking to herself.'

'I would have liked Charlie and Beth to come to my review but they didn't ask me, you see. And nobody phoned them afterwards. They wouldn't let me. I told her – asked – Community Nurse Brightside to ring, she said she hadn't time. She said she had to go home. Well, my meeting weren't while half past four anyway. I can't tell them what to do, can I? I don't want to get in trouble. I mean deputy could've done it because he were in my review.'

'They asked me if I wanted to go home and come back for weekends, for my tea and come back, or come back for a week and stay in hostel for a week and then go home again. And I said no. So I've had a letter from manager, it's in my bag. I'll be stopping here because they don't think I can get on with my husband. They said in that letter.'

'We don't get on so well. It's with them rowing, you see. It's me as well, I row. I admit it in that review last Wednesday. On about money all time when I haven't got any money. When Beth moves out I don't want to go back and live with Charlie because Charlie's going to get a smaller house. I still have feelings for him. He came on Thursday.'

'I should have gone home last Tuesday, but I had a review. Talking to me, what I wanted and that. I mean they were all talking at once, you know what I mean? Staff brought review letter to me. Yes, I agreed what was in letter. But I don't know what they said when I came out, you see. Letter's in my handbag, do you want to look at it?

'Well, if I go back and live with Charlie, it isn't just me, is it? They're all rowing and they're bringing me into it all time, and our Paul's going to talk to me when he sees me when I'm on my own, said so Saturday. Community Nurse Brightside said it's nowt to do with our Paul. Charlie and me didn't get on before, when Beth were in hospital. I don't know why she took those tablets. I remember when she were raped but that were ages since. Yes, I know what it's like because I've been raped myself, I should know. It happened before I got married to Charlie. I went out with somebody else. Yes, it was horrible. I got pregnant from that rape. I had Jonathan.'

'I'm going up home for my things today. My hi-fi and my stuff. You can't understand me, can you? Can't be helped, can it? I can't say I want to go and live with so-and-so. There isn't many who I know here.'

'Paul said he won't talk to me where people is. When our Paul talks to me it might upset me. He upset me before. You see, he blames me for it all. Nobody understands. Only them at church where I go. Well, I haven't talked to them about it.'

'Beth says Charlie wants a bungalow. Charlie'll have to get a home help but I don't think he'll be able to have home help because I couldn't. I saw him at club, I went Sunday and Saturday. No, I don't sit with him, he collects glasses, doesn't he? I sit with Beth.'

'Community Nurse Sharpe's getting a little nanny to look after little Edward. I haven't seen him. She were going to bring it to see me.'

A member of staff enters the room and Rosie introduces me as her friend. Rosie announces that she is going to phone home later and the woman reassures her there's no problem. I arrange to see Rosie in just under two weeks' time.

Monday in Rosie's flat. She makes me a cup of coffee as usual.

'Well, Community Nurse Brightside should've come Friday to take my blood pressure and nobody came. I waited in all morning and nobody phoned. Community Nurse Brightside were taking me to job centre Friday, I didn't get there neither. She rung in to say she were poorly but nobody rang to tell staff at flats she weren't coming.'

'I've been on my periods again, I come on last week again after all that time. I told my keyworker and she went for a pad and she come back and I started crying. It lasted for a few days. So I wonder if I'll have another, I might have, mighten I? I don't like telling a man about that, you see. Staff says I've got a man doctor, I can't choose, I've to have which will take me. I said, well, you can't really tell a man about your periods, can you?'

'I saw Paul, when he come home from work. I asked him to come and see me next Sunday, with being Mother's Day, and he says he doesn't like coming here. Beth comes, Charlie doesn't come. He's only been once when I were at hostel. He says he hasn't finished with me anyway. I don't know what I'm getting for Mother's Day, have to wait and see. Our Paul'll buy me summat but they'll give it me next Saturday, you see. Our Jonathan doesn't buy me owt. He doesn't buy owt for birthdays or Christmas. His divorce is going back to court. Don't see grandchildren much. It were Cathy's birthday. She were four last Friday. Guy, he's eight. Jonathan has them on Saturday, takes them to swimming baths, but he has to take them back at four o'clock. I used to go see his wife. We got on all right, but they used to be rowing. She used to sit in kitchen and he used to sit in room. Trouble started maybe when they had children. Our Jonathan used to work. He said to me last Monday, he says, if I wasn't silly I'd still have my job, wouldn't I?'

'Beth came yesterday. She had her tea with me. She brings her own tea. I'm seeing psychiatrist in two weeks again. Beth asked if they've to go. I says, ask Charlie to ring because I can't. I've to go to phone box, you see. Phone box is right down there across road. I wanted to ring you on Thursday, staff said to go to a phone box. It were dark. I went to somebody else's house who I know. It's silly that. You should be able to use phone if you pay for it. I'm going to ask deputy if I can use phone but he might not let me.'

I go with Rosie to the hostel office and the deputy says there's no problem about her using the phone. Rosie sees me to my car and I ask if she would like to come out with me for a meal next time we meet – and perhaps we can invite Charlie along, too. Rosie agrees, although, she says, I shall have to check with staff first.

I phone Rosie in the first week of April to let her know that Charlie has agreed to come with us for a meal. Rosie is to see the psychiatrist on Tuesday but, she says, Charlie and Beth won't be there. Community Nurse Brightside has told her that now they are all living separately there is no need for them to attend. Beth has already expressed a wish to go. I have a word with staff who agree that after 34 years of marriage her family do matter. In any case, the original idea had been for the family to talk through their difficulties with the consultant. They assure me they will say something to the community nurse.

On Tuesday I phone Charlie and confirm arrangements for the following week. He has put in for a single person's flat but would cancel if Beth wanted to move back home. Beth calls regularly to see him on a Monday and he cooks a meal for her. He also gives her a shepherd's pie to take home. He says he is fed up with asking Rosie to come back to him.

Rosie and Beth phone a bit later from a call box. She is upset after her meeting with the psychiatrist (no Beth or Charlie). She feels she is being blamed for arguments in the flat with Alice. Alice, she says, has threatened to throw her downstairs. Staff have refused Rosie use of the phone.

The next Tuesday I collect Rosie as arranged and then Charlie. We decide to eat at a café a few miles away. Rosie has been put on a diet of salads at the hostel but orders two sausages, egg and chips for lunch.

Rosie relates an incident that had happened at the weekend. She had suffered chest pains while at the club and Beth had phoned the hostel. The staff on night shift had said there was nothing they could do, so Beth had taken her mother to the hospital casualty department. Rosie had been examined and prescribed tablets. On returning to the hostel she found herself in trouble for going to hospital and 'wasting their time'. Staff have refused to give her the tablets.

We enjoy a friendly and happy meal together. Charlie is still very protective of Rosie and she still looks to him for guidance. We discuss Rosie's future and spell out all the options. Rosie knows what she doesn't want. She doesn't want to go home even if Charlie is not there, she doesn't want to go and live with friends, she doesn't want to live with Charlie in a new flat, she doesn't want to go with Beth, she doesn't want to have a flat where Beth comes to live with her. There's nobody she wants to live with but she doesn't want to live on her own.

Rosie asks if I will attend a review with her that has been arranged for ten days' time and I agree. I suggest that if the subject of her moving is on the agenda then we ought to have a quiet talk about it back at her place. We drop Charlie off at a friend's house – next time, he says, he's paying – and return to the hostel.

'No, I don't like living here. It's not just Alice. It's staff on to me all time. I asked unit manager about a flat, he says I can't have one. I don't know really if it's what I want. I asked to live on my own when I were at hostel, when I had that review. Unit manager says they're flats for people who's married, them who need them. I don't know, I've not really lived on my own. I told occupational therapist I want a flat on my own. She said I can't have one yet.'

Before leaving, I am convinced that Rosie would really like a flat for herself, given the right support. Out of curiosity, we go to the office and ask a staff member what tablets had been prescribed for her by the casualty doctor. They are painkillers.

Easter Saturday and Rosie phones. She is having tea with Charlie in her old house. She tells me that the following Tuesday she and Beth are going on a day trip to Bridlington and she is seeing her new doctor on Wednesday – a woman.

Friday, and the day of Rosie's review. Beth (whom I have invited along) and Rosie are in the flat waiting for me. Rosie has brought me a pottery cat from her trip and Beth gives me a pottery rabbit. Rosie produces an Easter egg and explains it's from Charlie. I am overwhelmed.

Downstairs in the office seven people gather for the review – Rosie, Beth, the Centre manager, the occupational therapist, the community nurse, a member of staff and I. The time of the review has been altered to accommodate the GP and nurse, but neither of them turns up. The Centre manager asks Rosie if she has requested the review as he doesn't know what it's about. Rosie says no. It seems the member of staff who has arranged it has decided to have the day off. As far as I can see the main purpose of the review is to chastise Rosie over her 'unsupervised' visit to the hospital. Nobody asks Beth about it at all. A general discussion ensues about Rosie's future. I am made to feel ostracized and a source of aggravation when making a comment. I ask Rosie if she would prefer to live on her own with support. She hesitates, bless her, and says she doesn't know.

The next day Rosie phones to ask what I thought of the review. She is now worried what the absent staff member will say when she returns on Monday. The day after, I go abroad for two weeks' holiday.

On the afternoon of my return Rosie phones to say her holiday has been arranged with people from the flats. They are going to Butlins at Skegness. She asks if I will come to her birthday party. A whole year has passed since we first met. I arrange to see her in two weeks' time.

Rosie shows me a copy of the report she has been sent about her review. It is a fair representation of events. Neither Beth nor I have been sent a copy.

'Staff say do this, do other, don't show me up on holiday, don't be poorly on holiday or you go back, don't be poorly else you won't be going and don't be sick neither. No, I'm not looking forward to my holiday.'

'I've got headaches all time. It all hurts up here. It's people getting on, upsetting me, people getting on to me, that's what doctor said. Staff says well, she isn't staying there long, she's going to another house. But I'm going to look round to see if I want to go there. Our Paul says he doesn't want me to have a flat on my own – because staff rung him last Tuesday and spoke to him.'

'I'm all right shopping. She writes me a list, Ann. No, I can't read it. I can remember what I want, you know. Ann comes to do a meal with me on a Friday now. I cook my own tea on a Friday. Do you know, my arm's gone dead.'

A member of staff enters the room and asks Rosie if she wants to go into town a bit later on to go to the bank and to buy some new shoes for her holiday. Rosie asks if she can have a new cardigan as well. The woman says unfortunately not and adds that she's lucky to be getting some shoes. We decide to finish in ten minutes.

'Silly woman! "Can't have a new cardigan"! She's finishing at four so what's good of taking me now. I'd have to rush round. So you're coming to my party then? Is your husband coming, yes?'

Ten days later I receive a postcard from Skegness, written by staff. 'Having a nice time . . . See you soon, Rosie'.

As soon as she returns from holiday, Rosie phones to say she has an appointment that Tuesday with the psychiatrist. She is excited because she has been told the new house is now ready. The next morning's post brings an invitation to her birthday party at the working men's club.

Mid-week at the Centre and Rosie is waiting in the hallway for me. She gives me a present from her holiday – a perfumed pink heart in lace. We sit together in the dining room. She has been on 'library duty' this morning: delivering and returning library books to old people in the community. She tells me that Charlie has been offered a one-bedroom flat and is wanting to move as soon as possible. Rosie knows she cannot go back now – she says it feels a bit strange.

'I've got nobody now. Community Nurse Sharpe only came to see me with that doctor, she hasn't been since. I saw her last week in car going to work. All she did is wave to me.'
    'I showed psychiatrist your [business] card and he says, "Is she a social worker?". I said no, she isn't. Talked about do I want to go to new house or do I want to go to another hostel. I said I don't know, I'm going to look at new house, see what it's like first. And then keyworker got on about I wanted to live on my own in a flat, and she says I'm not fit to live on my own. They say no, I need support, you know what I mean? But I didn't cry this time, I nearly did. Have you anything to ask doctor, she said. It'd been better for a community nurse had gone with me. You see keyworker doesn't really know me. Because she's only new. I says, well, could I ask Charlie and Beth to come? She said, "I didn't stop them coming". I said, can they come next time?
    Somebody told me the house were ready and now they tell me it's not. Don't know who to believe, do you? It's taking a long time, innit? I should have gone in July.'
    'Well, on my holiday I went out with staff and bought some new clothes. It were my last day nearly. I bought a new cardigan. Mary Miller started shouting at me and showing me up in pub, and when I got back she played 'ummer with me, started rowing and Wednesday morning she smothered, she put pillow over my head. So I told staff. Well I didn't want to sleep with her, you see. I said I'm going to sleep where television is. Staff said you're not, you're going to bed. I says I'm not. I'd to share a bed with her, you see, because it were a double bed. And staff come up, she said do you want me to take you back and put you in a police cell.'

    Six days later Rosie phones to say she has some bad news. She has been told she won't be moving into the new house. Someone else has been chosen to go. She tells me that Charlie and Paul are very angry at this decision. Charlie, she adds, has moved into his new flat and Beth, too, has been given a one-bedroom flat.
    The Birthday Party. This year it is held at the working men's club where Charlie helps out. Around the room are over 30 birthday cards and a pile of presents (among them a plate from Beth with the inscription, 'Mother, thanks for being wonderful and for all the things you do to make the world a better place just by being you'). Charlie and Paul have paid for an enormous birthday supper. It is a gloriously sunny evening and outside a few people are playing bowls in the lengthening shadows. Rosie's friends from the club and the church are there and Rosie introduces me to them all, especially Paul, her younger son. Rosie is upset that Community Nurse Brightside hasn't turned up. We dance, sing, play party games, talk,

eat and drink and then have our photos taken. Paul makes a thank-you speech on behalf of his mother. Rosie sits on one side of me and Beth the other.

We meet again about a week later at Rosie's hostel flat. Rosie and Charlie have now been married for 34 years. Rosie had bought Charlie another cigarette lighter and card, and Charlie had given Rosie a card and a mug.

'Charlie got me anniversary card. Our Paul's buying me summat later, and Sally. I'm still slimming, look. I nearly fell over, I lost my balance in Leeds on Saturday. I don't know when I'm moving. I go shopping on my own now. I can't read notice so I ask one of shop assistants and they go round with me.'

'I rang Sunday just to talk to you, that's all. Our Paul got mad with me other week. He says don't ring her up at weekends, she won't like it. So he tore your phone number up. Maybe he had a barney at work with somebody and took it out on me.'

'Chops, carrots and taties. No, I can't cook, staff did it. I do ironing at Centre – I iron table covers and tea towels. I don't like that Centre. Keyworker told me off because I wouldn't do any ironing. Three of them got on to me. I had to do it, she said. If you don't do it, get home, she said. I were crying. Manager took me in office. I can get on with manager.'

'I've asked to go to hospital but they won't let me. (Rosie cries.) It's my fingers hurt me all time. I daren't go because when I went before I got in trouble, didn't I? You see, I haven't got a community nurse now. I can't go to my doctor on my own. Staff has to go with me. They're saying I'm going every week, "See how you go, there's nobody to take you". Community Nurse Brightside used to take me. Nurse Sharpe'd never take me, she says she hasn't time. I haven't seen baby Edward yet. It's not fair. Everybody's got a photo of him except me.'

'I bought myself a bread board. I've to save it when I move from here. Do you know where Paul's going to live? Other side of Wakefield. There's only me next, isn't there? I asked deputy last night when I'm moving and he said he doesn't know. I should have gone now, July's gone now. I asked staff if a flat comes empty can I go and live on my own. She said, if one comes empty. She said, "You won't be here long". Community Nurse Brightside says she'd come and see me before I went on my holidays, she didn't come. She didn't come to my party neither and she didn't even ring up to tell me. Ah well, ne'er mind.'

'Take me with you. I want to go to your house one day. I mean it. I'd like to stay with you. You see, I haven't got a community nurse now (crying). I can't ring, they've stopped me ringing down there now because staff said they've had a big phone bill from Social Services. Staff says it's not for that, it's for emergencies like doctors and that.'

As I leave Rosie asks me to come with her to see the deputy while she asks about moving. The deputy says that nothing has been decided yet. They thought the house she was originally going to move into would be better occupied by a 'quieter' group. I explain to Rosie that from Friday I shall be on a month's holiday.

The Sunday evening following my return to work the phone rings. It is Rosie and Beth phoning together from the club, just to say hallo.

Two days later I phone Rosie at the flats. She says she's missed me. She has been told that the hostel is closing down soon and she will be moving out, although no date has been given. Rosie says she wants a flat on her own. Beth took an overdose again three weeks ago but has now started on a course at the local college. Jonathan has been banned from visiting her because he had entered one of the other flats without permission. The previous evening she had been hit on the back by two young lads while out shopping. She becomes upset and cries. Someone had seen her to the hostel and explained what had happened to staff who had recorded the incident in a book. I arrange to take her into town for a coffee next Tuesday.

She is still getting ready when I arrive. Beth and some church friends are coming later that afternoon to take her out for tea. We drive into town, have a coffee and then go shopping for Beth's birthday present. Rosie says she hasn't much money but it's the thought that counts. She takes me to some discount shops to look for pens but nothing catches her eye. We spot some large glass fruit bowls and Rosie asks me the price. One pound. She can't believe how cheap they are and asks me to check again. In the end she buys two, one for Beth and one for herself. We wander back to the car looking in shop windows, and Rosie instinctively links my arm every time we cross a road. She talks non-stop until I drop her off at the hostel.

A fortnight later a letter comes from Rosie, written by Beth. She hopes I am keeping well. She has another appointment to see the psychiatrist. She thanks me for taking her out. She is now working an extra day at the Salvation Army which is what she has wanted. She hopes to see me soon and asks me to write back. I send a cautious reply – aware that it will probably be read to her by staff – and suggest we meet on Tuesday.

Rosie greets me outside her flat with a broad smile. I am suddenly conscious of how much weight she has lost. She tells me she is now 10 st. 10 lb., down almost 3 stones. Her face has become quite lined and her skirts are loose. She also looks a lot older. Alice has been moved out of the flat and she has a new companion, Mavis. Mavis has been chosen as someone Rosie might live with in the future.

'Staff says I haven't to go on a diet no more. I just get ordinary now. Staff's complaining because I can't keep my clothes up now.'

'I don't want to live with Mavis. I told staff. It's up to me that, isn't it? She's taking my money. And my cereals and my bread. I didn't want to tell.

Staff says, it's a good job you did. I told staff I want to live on my own. Somebody said you can't go live on your own. I don't know who it was, it was staff. Our Paul says I can't live on my own.'

'If kids hit me and I told staff, they say, oh we can't do owt about it. But staff are there to look after you, that's what our Paul said, that's what they get paid for. They put it in a book but they don't do owt about it. A kid were going to knife me. But if they cut my head open what would they have to do? I can't go to hospital on me own, I'd have to go tell staff, wouldn't I? I can't go to police, I'll get in trouble. I've got a headache, it's all up here.'

'Staff were with her husband shopping in supermarket and she came up to me, she didn't tell me off, she just told me I should have told them I couldn't read. She said shop assistants shouldn't have been going round with me, they shouldn't be helping me.'

A week later I receive a letter from Rosie, written by Beth. She has checked out with the staff at the Centre and they have agreed that I can phone her there if necessary. Her son, Paul, is moving house on Friday and Beth is taking her to a pie and pea supper. She ends by saying: 'I'll be glad when I leave the hostel and move into my own house. I will be my own boss then. Please write back.'

It is now early November and I meet Rosie at her hostel flat.

'I told unit manager what you told me to tell her about these lads won't leave me alone when I come home from Centre. And I said, I'm complaining to you. She says, I'm not for complaints. Unit manager says if they cut my head open there'll be serious trouble, that's what she said, that's all she said. I've told Centre staff about it. She said: "Why don't you tell your keyworker?" I said I've told them but she doesn't take any notice. She's too young really.'

'Yes, I've seen our Paul's house, it's a big 'un. I can get bus 253 on at South Hill and then they meet me other end. Because I'd get lost, you see, on my own. Beth'll be coming to see me tomorrow night, seven o'clock. On Sunday she goes to her dad's for her dinner and on a Wednesday she comes here. Charlie's asked me to go but, you see, it's dark now at nights and, as I told him, with kiddies picking on me it's not wise to go out on my own. I cried last Tuesday, got upset. I swore at staff because, you see, our Beth, she used Mavis's boiled ham and she thought it were mine. And I got in trouble for it, didn't I? Staff came and told me off an' all up here. Staff said you can do your own tea, I'm not doing it no more.'

'Our Beth's on about getting married and having two babies. Getting engaged and he's getting a car and she's getting married. You don't get married straightaway, you've got to get to know people, haven't you? I've been to Charlie's for tea but he goes out to club and I don't like going drinking a lot you see. I go Saturday when there's a turn on. You see, with high blood pressure nurse told me you hadn't to have too much beer, have you? I leave at half past ten.

'I got played 'ummer with because I bought ornament and it were too

much. I bought it out of catalogue over there, at hostel, and she said it were too much but I've paid for it now.'
   'Don't know when I'm moving from here. They says they're not ready yet. I've asked to live on my own.'

The last Sunday in November and Rosie phones me from the club. She has recently been accosted by two youths on the way home again. We arrange to go out for a Christmas drink in a fortnight's time. This is the last time I shall visit Rosie as a researcher. We have agreed we would both like to stay in touch, although Rosie realizes that my work will prevent me from seeing her so often.
   It is 14 December and I arrive at Rosie's flat a little after 7.00 p.m. I can see her watching through the curtains for me. She greets me at the door and immediately hands over Christmas presents and cards. A box of chocolates from Beth and a vanity bag and accessories from her. She puts my card and present in her room along with others she has been given. So far she has 15 cards. She asks if this is the last time we shall see each other. The first of many times she asks the same question. Each time I give her the same answer: that I shall keep in touch. She says she will miss me.
   Rosie calls in at the office to tell staff we are going out. As we are driving into town we see a man pushing a bike up the hill on the other side of the road. Rosie exclaims: 'It's Jonathan!' The only member of her family I have not met. Rosie asks me to stop and she opens the door as we draw up alongside him. We are introduced. Rosie tells him she has bought her grandchildren selection boxes for Christmas. Jonathan asks for Paul's new address and Rosie says she doesn't know. (Paul has asked her not to give it as Jonathan is always asking him for money.) We say goodbye. Rosie tells me that she used to visit him regularly in the children's home but had found it difficult once the other children were born. She had become closer to him when, as an adult, he had started to visit her.
   We find a warm and cosy pub, although it is virtually empty. Rosie has a small beer and some crisps. We talk for over an hour and Rosie follows up with a large cream sherry. We celebrate.
   Back at her flat, she asks if I will be going to her birthday party next year. I say I will if she invites me, but add that I will see her long before then. She touches me on the arm and then walks away quickly. Turning at the door, she waves.

CHAPTER 8

Reading Rosie Spencer

Why should we be interested in Rosie Spencer? What insights can one person's story provide into the experience of other parents? After all, even among the small number of parents in our study, she is rather special. A grandmother, with three adult children, two daughters-in-law and two grandchildren, she also, uniquely, chose to move out of the family home to live first in a local authority hostel and later alone. Yet her story as told helps to throw light on what it means to be a parent with learning difficulties. Rosie Spencer may not be typical of other parents, but parents like her typically face the same kinds of problems and pressures in their lives. By looking beyond what is particular to her as a person, the common threads that run through the experience of all such parents may be picked out and examined. The story of any other family in the study would have served the purpose equally well. Rosie Spencer more or less chose herself.

The life story approach reveals social relations in action. Rosie Spencer occupies a niche within society defined by her role as a mother with learning difficulties. She occupies this niche along with other parents similarly labelled. By looking into her personal history it is possible to see at work the wider social forces that bear more generally on people in her position and shape their lives. The nature of these forces and pressures is exposed by the imprint they leave on an individual's biography.

Like most people with learning difficulties, Rosie Spencer has a lot of people meddling in her life and assuming the right to order her about. Similarly, too, she lacks the kinds of resources – money, status, friends in the right places, words, self-confidence – with which to defend herself against the capricious exercise of power by those in authority over her. Her personal experience provides a window on to the operation of the health and welfare services and the way in which parents with learning difficulties are treated. The details of her story are unique to her case but the form of her dealings and relationships with practitioners reveals the underlying values that inform professional practice with parents like her.

Outside her immediate circle of family and friends, Rosie Spencer is regarded more as a cipher than a character in her own right or a fellow citizen. Service workers ignore her role as a parent and grandparent and see only a woman with learning difficulties; a volunteer looks on her as a child; the law assigns her a separate status on the grounds of severe mental impairment; neighbourhood kids treat her as fair game, a target for their pranks and abuse, while the police fail to take her complaints seriously. Too few people rise above their prejudices to see the person behind the label. It is precisely because Rosie Spencer is so often seen as a stereotype rather than as an individual that her experiences mirror those of other parents with learning difficulties and lead us to a fuller understanding of their lives.

As an account of her family life, Rosie Spencer's story shows how much we have yet to learn about being a parent with learning difficulties. Like any biography, it also illuminates her times and provides an angle of vision on society at large. Most research has followed a single-track approach and asked only what effects people's learning difficulties have on their family life and their competence as parents. Little attempt has been made to look in the other direction at the way society structures the kind of life parents with learning difficulties are able to lead. A feature of Rosie Spencer's story is how little the fact of her having learning difficulties intrudes on her private life. It is simply not germane to those who are close to her. Her label is primarily a convenience by which agencies and public officials regulate their formal relations with her as their client. It is for this reason that studies of individual lives have much to tell us about the ways in which the institutions and practices of a society are perceived and experienced by parents with learning difficulties and how they influence the course of their lives.

The story has been compiled from edited extracts of 20 taped interviews, the notes of unrecorded conversations, and information and material from other sources including 66 phone calls, letters, postcards, photographs, meetings, visits, social gatherings and outings. It is a distillation of more than 100 hours spent in Rosie Spencer's company over a period of 18 months. And still we are left wanting to know more about her. For instance, along with the rest of her family, we never did get to the bottom of why she went to live in the hostel, and resisted Charlie's entreaties to return home even though she disliked the place. If intensive research of this kind serves to highlight the complexities of people's lives, it also raises important questions about the limitations of clipboard and checklist methods based on brief, one-off interviews or observational snapshots. Dowdney and Skuse (1993), for example, report that work on the observational assessment of parenting behaviour and its relationship to child development has so far been based on observational periods of between three and ten minutes. The lesson of Rosie Spencer's story is that parenting cannot be reduced to a set of tick boxes or rendered in terms of numbers alone. There is a need to move beyond blanket descriptions of parents with learning difficulties that allow them no say in their own destiny. People's qualities as parents are more surely revealed in their lived lives than by standardized assessment schedules or behavioural tests.

What shines through Rosie's narrative is how much her family means to her and, just as importantly, how much she means to her family. They have had their ups and downs, and still do, but their relationships have stood the test of time. Indeed, as a family, they have taken more knocks than most – and survived when others might have cracked. The depth of these emotional ties is only occasionally and tangentially evoked by them in words; it is more clearly seen in their actions. Also it only becomes apparent from a close knowledge of the family history and from seeing them together in different situations. This sort of understanding calls for intensive methods of research such as the life story approach (and also for practitioners who have a long-term involvement in the family). Research or practice devoid of such familiarity runs the risk of seriously misrepresenting the quality of parenting provided by people with learning difficulties as well as the nature of their family life. Of course, it is not possible to draw any clear-cut conclusions about parents in general from a single case: except perhaps one. Rosie Spencer alerts us to the danger of making easy generalizations on the basis of a superficial knowledge of parents as people.

As well as holding up a mirror to society, the personal story as a tool of research also provides an inner view of the person. In so doing, as Birren and Hedlund (1987) have explained, it offers clues to the adaptive strategies used by individuals in coping with the demands of life that can neither be 'tested in the laboratory nor gleaned from questionnaires'. The life story also provides an insight into people's perceptions of their own needs. Services for parents with learning difficulties are determined primarily by managers and practitioners, usually without reference to the parents' viewpoint (Walton-Allen and Feldman 1991). For instance, there is known to be a discrepancy between professional and parental perspectives on what constitutes adequate parenting (Llewellyn 1991). Walton-Allen and Feldman (1991) found that mothers felt they were being over-serviced in some areas but under-serviced in others. In particular, they received more assistance than they felt was necessary in all areas of child care and less than they wanted in personal relations, vocational and assertiveness training, and communication skills. As Thompson (1992) has noted in the case of older people, those aspects of their lives which are not highly valued by external observers may well be among the most significant in terms of their own sense of self. It is how individuals compose their own reality that is the essence of their needs (Johnson 1976). The life story can provide access to this subjective view of the world as a counterweight to an otherwise one-sided reliance on professional opinion.

These are some of the reasons why the life story as a method of research deserves our attention, and why Rosie Spencer's story bears examination as an example of the genre. Our purpose is not to test hypotheses or generate theory, but simply to draw out some of the key themes and issues that emerge from her story as a pointer to future practice and research.

Life stories may be viewed as a *resource* or a *topic* (Bowker 1993). As a resource, providing data about the real world, the focus is on the dynamics of lives as revealed in the content of the stories. As a topic for analysis, the focus is on the dynamics of narration and the process by which accounts of lives are produced and turned into text. The practice lessons of Rosie Spencer's story come from treating it as a resource. The lessons for research are more clearly seen when it is regarded as a topic in its own right.

Rosie Spencer's story as a resource

Practice pointer 1: Be wary of assuming that parents with learning difficulties do not have the same feelings of care and affection for their children as other parents or that their family bonds are weaker.

Galliher (1973) notes that one of the reasons often given for doubting the parental fitness of people with learning difficulties is their supposed inability to 'supply an adequate measure of love and affection'. Feldman et al. (1989) also cite several studies that have found such mothers less likely to be affectionate, responsive and accommodating to their children. The implication seems to be that emotional feelings are somehow linked to intelligence. This way of thinking is evident in some of the actions and decisions by professionals in Rosie's case: for example, the community nurse's refusal to discuss Rosie's anxieties about her daughter; the failure to invite either Charlie or Beth to Rosie's review or to let them know the outcome; and the playing down of Rosie's specific request for a family appointment with the psychiatrist. Each of these incidents points to the reluctance of staff to accept that these family relationships matter.

Anyone listening to Rosie Spencer would soon realize that her family, and especially her children, are central to what she holds most dear. Despite the fact that, in the face of internal and external pressures on the family, Rosie chose to live apart from her husband and daughter, she has remained in almost daily contact with them and continues to look to them for companionship, affirmation and support.

The relationship between Charlie and Rosie has survived the arguments that separated them. They remain intensely loyal to one another, and both take pride in the number of years they have been married. They still search out each other's company, whether at the club on weekends or at Charlie's house for tea. Birthdays and anniversaries are celebrated together.

In the event, the family has negotiated some testing changes quite successfully. Beth's wanting to leave home undoubtedly put a lot of pressure on Rosie and Charlie. On the one hand, she made an important contribution to the smooth running of the household – both as the only literate member able to handle paperwork and by doing the shopping and ironing and sharing the other domestic chores with her father. On the other hand, her parents felt she was too vulnerable and naive in her outlook on life to live on her own safely. The tension between these concerns, their own self-interest and Beth's wishes led to fierce family rows that culminated in the break-up of the home. Yet together they have managed to establish a new routine based on reciprocity and family values. Beth continues to help her father with his housework, and to handle her mother's correspondence when she visits her at the hostel. Charlie always makes a meal for Beth once a week and gives her a shepherd's pie to take home. Rosie sometimes lends Beth money, although she herself has little to spare, and has obtained furniture and equipment for her from the Salvation Army.

Although the Spencer family are not given to outward shows of affection, as most clearly evidenced on the hospital visit following Beth's overdose, there are abundant examples of the kinship and love between them: in Charlie's eloquent portrayal of his feelings for Rosie; in Rosie and Charlie's worry and tears over their daughter; in the regular day trips Rosie and Beth share together; and in the weekly visits Rosie makes to see her son, Paul, and his wife. Only Jonathan, the first son, who was in care almost from birth until 18, lacks a place in the family circle, though Rosie still makes an effort to stay in contact and always buys Christmas and birthday presents for her grandchildren. As with most families, the children have been a source of both torment and joy. Indeed, Beth can still cause her mother upset and aggravation when minded. The two younger children in particular, though, are loving and protective towards their mother, as instanced by Paul's assault on his father when Charlie was once contemplating a divorce, Beth's gift of an inscribed plate (which Rosie keeps on display in her window-sill) and Paul's spontaneous tribute at her birthday party.

The most remarkable thing about the Spencers is that the family bonds have held fast under pressures that would have shattered the relationships in many families with apparently greater coping resources: initial opposition to Rosie and Charlie's marriage from professionals and extended family alike; a first child from a rape; accusations of child abuse against Charlie; the removal into care of all the children for many years; Rosie's institutionalization for extended periods; Paul's brief imprisonment; Beth's attempted suicides; and, finally, Rosie's decision to live apart from Charlie. Despite all these trials, their marriage has lasted 34 years and, even though they are living separately for the moment, as has happened before, there is no sign that they can do without each other. Rosie remains a paradox: the linchpin of the family as well as a source of much of its travail. Without her the other members would likely go their own ways. Without them she would probably become just another lonely person in a local authority hostel.

Practice pointer 2:   Parenting is about more than childrearing.
Practice pointer 3:   Be wary of adopting too narrow a view of the parenting task.

As Llewellyn (1991) has urged, 'it is incumbent upon professionals working with parents to explore and clarify the meaning they give to adequate parenting'. Research in this area provides little help. Fotheringham (1980) concludes that children of parents with learning difficulties face 'an increased risk of experiencing an unstimulating environment with limited opportunities for learning' and that few parents are likely to provide 'conditions of care at the minimal acceptable level'. Contrary to such a prediction, Feldman et al. (1985) found the quality of their home environments fell within the average range. Similarly, where Floor et al. (1975) find no reason why people with learning difficulties should not take on the responsibilities of parenthood, Accardo and Whitman (1990) see the relevant question regarding parenting failure as being 'not whether but when'. A key factor accounting for these varying conclusions is the lack of attention that has been given to how the concept of adequate parenting should be defined and measured (Dowdney and Skuse 1993).

Three features of the research to date stand out. It has focused on those aspects of parenting behaviour that are most easily observed, quantified and measured such as caretaking skills, the use of discipline, and the provision of cognitive stimulation (primarily through play). The emphasis has been on assessing parenting deficits and the incidence of parenting breakdown as measured in terms of developmental delays (especially in language) in the children, their removal into care or the extent of maltreatment, neglect and abuse. In contrast to this preoccupation with the negative aspects of parenting by people with learning difficulties (Tymchuk 1992), virtually no consideration has been given to the special strengths they display in managing to cope at all under the variety and severity of pressures they face in their everyday lives (Czukar 1983). Lastly, all the available evidence − mostly gleaned from early intervention programmes – refers to infants and young children. There have been no studies of older or adult children. Consequently, we have no knowledge of the longer-term effects on personal adjustment of being brought up by parents with learning difficulties, of the nature of the relationships between parents and their adult children or of how the parents themselves negotiate their transition through the family life cycle.

Rosie Spencer's story demonstrates what all mothers and fathers find out eventually: that parenting does not end when the children grow up. Rosie still worries about all hers, shares in their upsets and achievements, is involved in their lives, keeps an eye on them, offers support when she can and values their affection. Like many parents with grown-up children, she is also the conduit for family news. She is proud of how well Paul has done for himself and was pleased for him and his wife when they moved into a bigger house, but anxious about how far he now had to journey to work. Jonathan, her eldest son, is a cause of concern. She despairs at his foolishness in losing his job for hitting the foreman, and feels sorry about his marriage failing, although she knows the rowing was no good for the children who have reached an age to understand. She disapproves of his rudeness towards Sally, his sister-in-law, and the way he sponges off Paul. When Jonathan asked for his brother's new address Rosie pleaded ignorance to prevent him from pestering them for money. Although she feels hurt that he forgets her birthday, and knows he has behaved badly towards her at times, stealing money and causing her embarrassment by getting himself banned from the hostel, she has nevertheless stood by him as his mother. Rosie is perhaps closest to Beth, although their relationship is sometimes a stormy one. Beth will shout at her mother, call her names and, occasionally, even hit her. These episodes disturb Rosie profoundly, so much so that once the whole church prayed for her. Since Beth found her own home these flare-ups have happened much less often. They still spend a lot of time with each other, going places and doing things together. Rosie has cried the night away over Beth's attempts at suicide. As a rape victim herself, Rosie can sympathize with the feelings that have driven Beth to the edge of despair but, even so, she cannot understand why Beth should want to kill herself. She knows that Beth needs more help than she can give but does not know where to find it as her own workers will not accept that her family problems have anything to do with them. Overall, then, Rosie's story conveys a picture of someone very much wrapped up in her own family and its affairs who, much like other parents (and grandparents) of her age, is living at least part of her life through her children.

Rosie's story also reminds us that there is more to parenting than merely practical skills: the quality of parenting also depends on the qualities of the parent. Most intervention programmes in this field are geared specifically towards improving mothering through training in child care, homemaking and domestic skills, health and safety in the home, and play and interactional skills (Tymchuk 1990a). While all these skills are important, especially for single parents, Rosie's experience warns against making gendered assumptions about who does what in the home; failing to look at the family as a unit; equating parental competence with mothering skills; and overlooking the non-nurturing side of parenting.

Rosie Spencer has never been able to manage even basic child care or domestic tasks. Afraid of harming the children, they were a year old before she picked them up. Charlie assumed sole responsibility for all their day-to-day needs, except for teaching Rosie how to change their nappies when he switched from towelling to disposable ones. From the beginning, he received no guidance or support from the services – even having to ask how to make up a bottle. The fact that twenty years later he still recalls with pride how the clinic nurse commented on the whiteness of his nappies bears witness to the way he applied himself to the task. There has never been any suggestion that the children were less than adequately looked after. When, at the ages of nine and ten, they were taken into care, it was because of a (vigorously denied) allegation of cruelty, not neglect. Rosie did what little she could to help around the house, mainly cleaning, running errands, popping out to the shops. After coming home at 15, Beth helped her parents with the housekeeping and other chores. Charlie always did the cooking and managed the money.

As a mother, then, Rosie Spencer does not match up well against two important measures – childrearing and homemaking – of the parental task. Importantly, however, Charlie and Rosie as a team succeeded in meeting their children's needs together, and the family as a unit succeeded in keeping house at least up to the standards of their neighbours.

Practice pointer 4: Assessment, intervention and support must have regard to the functioning of the family as a unit.

Rosie's weaknesses are manifest, her strengths less tangible but none the less real. What she contributed to the parenting task were not skills but her qualities as a person. Parenting is about socialization as well as nurturing: it involves teaching, primarily by example, moral rules and values of social conduct. Consider the following qualities she displays in her story as told:

- *Kindness and generosity*: as shown, for example, by her sending of cards and giving of presents (to Community Nurse Brightside on her leaving, to Community Nurse Sharpe's new baby, to us on her return from holiday) even though she has little money.
- *Community spirit*: as shown, for example, by her involvement in her local church; the sense of reward she gets from her part in providing a library

service for housebound old people; her enjoyment of her voluntary work with the Salvation Army; and her taking a hot meal on Sundays to an infirm neighbour.

- *Sense of right and wrong*: as shown, for example, by her disapproval of Jonathan's ill-mannered behaviour towards Sally; her belief that staff should honour the promises they make; her reproaching Beth for going out with an old boyfriend while engaged to another.
- *Moral reasoning*: as shown, for example, by her understanding of staff's petty attitude towards her use of the office phone and her appreciation of the 'no-win' position into which she is put by official responses to her harassment by local youths.
- *Personal loyalty*: as shown, for example, by Charlie's comment that she'd be the first to stand up for him if ever he were in trouble, and her keeping in contact with Jonathan throughout his long years in care.
- *Sense of humour*: as shown, for example, by her frequent jokey references to Community Nurse Sharpe's brusqueness.
- *Perceptiveness*: as shown, for example, by her cautioning Beth to get to know her boyfriend better before she started talking about getting married and having babies.
- *Sensitivity and responsiveness to others*: as shown, for example, by wanting to visit Beth every day when she was in hospital, and her concern about the effects of Jonathan's failing marriage on the children.
- *Sense of personal dignity and worth*: as shown, for example, by her indignation at being referred to as a child by the Salvation Army volunteer, for being told tartly not to look out of the window by Community Nurse Sharpe, and when a social worker wanted to discuss her confidential affairs in a corridor.

This list illustrates some of Rosie's qualities as a person that are easily overlooked when assessing her competence as a parent. These qualities are an important aspect of parenting behaviour but rarely receive attention alongside the more practical skills, possibly because they only emerge on close acquaintance. As Charlie said, you've really got to live with a person like Rosie before you experience her good points.

Rosie Spencer's special accomplishments as a mother deserve emphasis because many parents fail to achieve as much even without the limitations and pressures she has had to face. Foremost among these achievements is maintaining a close and mutually valued relationship with Beth and Paul into adulthood. Although she played only a minor part in their upbringing as children she has now become the star of the family around whom the other members gravitate. This underlines, once again, the importance of taking a longer-term view of the family life cycle. Rosenberg and McTate (1982), for example, comment on the difficulty that parents with learning difficulties have 'in adjusting parenting styles to changes in their child's development'. Rosie Spencer's story alerts us to the transitory nature of this problem and to another lesson for practice:

Practice pointer 5: The parent–child relationship may be worth supporting even when a parent cannot meet all the developmental needs of the child.

Rosie's achievement, however, goes beyond simply remaining on good terms with her children. For she also had to help reconstitute the family after it was broken up when Beth and Paul were taken into care. Piecing together relationships after five years, when the children left as juniors and came back as teenagers, especially given all the trauma surrounding their removal, is hard enough. Even more remarkable is the fact that her eldest son, Jonathan, who was placed in care when he was only a month old, started to visit her when he moved out on his own at 18 and continued to do so after he married. The survival of the family speaks a lot for people's desire for a sense of attachment, security and place. As Judge Berman affirmed in the Colorado court of appeals, the state can substitute more easily for any deficiencies in a child's developmental needs 'than it can the love of a parent for its child, and of a child for its parent' (quoted in Gilhool and Gran 1985).

Practice pointer 6: The need for belonging on the part of children may outweigh any deficits that outsiders see in the competence of their parents.

For all her positive qualities and achievements as a parent, the health and welfare services responded to Rosie only as someone with learning difficulties. She became a victim of their unwitting discrimination. As a woman with learning difficulties, her only access to help was through services designated for her 'client group'. Yet, as a wife and a mother, these services were not designed to accommodate her needs.

When trouble flared at home, and Rosie needed time to think, she was placed in a hostel although her need was for a refuge. The hostel staff welcomed her as another pair of hands to help with the daily routine. They lacked both the insight and the skills to help Rosie to sort herself out: unable to see the importance of her family, they failed to grasp it was the reason for her leaving home. Rosie herself was viewed as the problem. Living in the hostel served to distance her even more from the family – both Charlie and Paul were loath to visit – while staff contrived to shut them out by, for example, failing to invite them to her reviews or to attend her meetings with the consultant psychiatrist. Although field staff were aware of her home situation, because Rosie had told them, they did not regard her family pressures as their concern. As the community nurse said, the family would have to sort them out for themselves. For Rosie, the price of moving into the hostel was a loss of personal autonomy. When she chose not to return home after her first review, Charlie suspected it was because she had already become institutionalized.

Practice pointer 7: Beware of seeing parents' needs only in terms of their learning difficulties.

Practice pointer 8: Beware of the danger of segregated services leading to segregated needs and segregated lives.

As a parent with learning difficulties, Rosie Spencer occupies an ambivalent status. In her role as a parent, she performs a valued task that is accorded respect, carries responsibility, calls for judgement and presumes a capacity for independent decision-making. As a person with learning difficulties, she is stigmatized, denied equal rights of citizenship, and labelled as incompetent, dependent and in need of protection. In the former guise she functions as a member of her family and the community, in the latter she appears as a service user or client. Coping with the contradictory pressures of these two life worlds is a major source of stress. An understanding of these pressures can be gleaned from her story.

As a family/community member, Rosie	*As a service user, Rosie*
can be assertive	is seen as difficult
sticks up for herself	must accept authority
expresses disagreement	must be compliant
makes her own decisions	must ask permission
can do things her way	must play by the rules
exercises discretion	is told what to do
is listened to	is fobbed off
is taken seriously	is patronized
is granted respect	is stigmatized
looks after her own money	has to account to staff
gives and takes	is cast as a recipient only
negotiates with others	obeys instructions
shoulders responsibility	is treated as dependent
is socially engaged	is a lone individual

Charlie is all too well aware of these conflicting pressures on Rosie. As he says to her: 'You see, when you're in the hostel, Rosie, you've to go by their rules . . . at home, you go by your own rules.' He also knows she finds them hard to handle at times. Her compunction to tell the community nurse 'every little thing' she does – 'as though she's the gaffer, sort of thing, that's over her' – is a constant source of frustration for the family. 'She's different with someone in authority. Me or Beth, we're not authority, you see, we just live in the same household, sort of thing.'

Practice pointer 9: Practitioners should take care not to undermine the socially valued aspects of the parenting role.

Practice pointer 10: Practitioners should organize services and support so that parents experience being competent and feel in control.

Rosie Spencer's preoccupation with her health is wearing for her family and practitioners alike. Charlie concedes it causes a good bit of friction with Beth, and that even he finds it irritating at times. He tells how she rings the community nurses 'nearly every day, telling them some type of story and one thing and another'. They, in turn, have blocked her access to her GP and allow her only one accompanied visit every six weeks. Whitman et al. (1989) have commented on the tendency of parents with learning difficulties to overtax their support network (see also Rosenberg and McTate 1982) and certainly Rosie appears to be exhausting everyone's reserves of patience and sympathy.

Her health problems have to be seen in the wider context of her life. Many of the minor accidents and ailments of which she complains could be treated at home with over-the-counter remedies, except that she cannot read health books and her knowledge of home medicine is too meagre for her to distinguish what needs attention from what does not. She has been diagnosed as having high blood pressure and advised to take her medication regularly or risk, as she puts it, 'a blood clot on the brain'. Her symptoms of headaches, nosebleeds, dizziness and blackouts are linked in her own mind with this condition. As an older woman, they may raise fears about her own mortality which she is unable to express in any other way. Also her health worries have coincided with her going through the menopause. Finally, Rosie has experienced numerous other stresses in her life during this period that may have contributed to her anxieties, including: relationship problems at home; problems over money; harassment and abuse in the neighbourhood, ranging from name-calling to physical assault; worries about her children (especially, latterly, about Beth's overdosing); and, recently, the pressures of communal living and a restrictive hostel regime.

It is too easy to see Rosie's demands on the health services as unreasonable and a sign of a general inability to cope. Given the multiplicity and seriousness of the stresses in her life, and her relative lack of coping resources (including knowledge, skills and negotiable possessions like money), it is inevitable that she, and others like her, will be driven to depending more on the abilities of others in order to exert a measure of control over their lives.

Practice pointer 11: Service providers must be ready to accept that parents with learning difficulties are likely to exert heavy demands on their resources.

If Rosie Spencer has leaned heavily on the health and welfare services in the past few years (as Charlie points out, they received very little when the children were small), it is equally true that they, in turn, have caused her a lot of problems. As McConachie (1991) has argued, 'services must realise the potential stresses they impose on families'.

These stresses are manifold and arise for a variety of reasons including: sundry assorted workers, frequently changing; contradictory advice; lack of co-ordination; loss of privacy; constant surveillance; broken promises; red tape and system abuse; bad practice; unqualified and/or inexperienced staff; discriminatory attitudes; and downright pettiness. Rosie Spencer has a stream of workers and professionals involved in her life, and most of their faces changed in the course of the study. There is her GP and practice nurse, her community nurse, the social education centre staff and keyworker, the hostel staff and keyworker, and a unit manager (all of whom changed), as well as a psychiatrist and registrar, her occupational therapist and her social worker. In addition, there are also workers involved with other members of the family: Beth was assigned a social worker after her overdose and subsequently began seeing a counsellor to work through her rape trauma, while Charlie had his own psychiatric nurse to help him cope with the emotional aftermath of the family rows prior to Beth and Rosie's leaving home and the death of his father. Rosie harbours no illusions about her need for support, but she does complain loudly about the terms on which it is delivered and the way she is treated. Looked at more closely, her story illustrates many common features of the services apparent in the experience of study parents:

- *A reactive style*: responding to problems and crises as and when they happen, dealing with their presenting symptoms rather than the underlying causes, and tackling them serially rather than holistically. Interestingly, this mirrors how Rosie herself views the troubles that afflict her – as one damned thing after another – without perceiving their linkages. An example of this approach is the review held after Rosie visited the hospital casualty department without permission. No attempt was made to probe more deeply into her health anxieties and to question whether they were being treated helpfully and effectively.
- *A resource-driven approach*: Rosie's needs have only ever been assessed in relation to the services available for people with learning difficulties.

Consequently, she has been shoehorned into facilities – like the hostel and the social education centre and the community mental handicap unit – that reinforce her identity as someone different, erode her status as a wife and mother, leave her dissatisfied, and close off consideration of less discriminatory alternatives (such as counselling to deal with the family problems and a proper job).

- *A lack of user involvement*: Rosie has been treated as a passive recipient of services and denied any real voice in her own welfare. She was given just a day's notice to pack and move into the hostel – take it or leave it – and the pros and cons of this step were never discussed with her. She has consistently expressed her dislike of the social education centre, emphasizing her feelings forcefully at her review, but no action has been taken to explore alternatives. Perhaps the surest sign of her compliance with the client role she has been assigned is her continuing attendance at the social education centre against her own wishes. On more than one occasion, Rosie was promised accommodation outside the hostel, without first being given an opportunity to view it, only to find out later that someone else had been allocated her place. Rosie's lack of involvement is not confined to big resource decisions: even her diet sheet was kept in a form that only staff could read and understand.

- *Poor targeting and co-ordination*: Rosie Spencer receives a lot of support but too little of it shows any clear plan or purpose. Even her review was missing an agenda – while the convenor took the day off 'in lieu'. Although staff recognized that Rosie would need help to achieve her wish of living on her own, there was no concerted effort to address her skill deficits. On Fridays, she was given training in cooking and shopping from an occupational therapist but her learning was not reinforced by other staff during the rest of the week. Meals were cooked for her and she was sent shopping with a list she could not read (and then reprimanded for asking a shop assistant for help – as she had been doing all her life).

- *Complacency and buck-passing*: these features show themselves by practitioners taking the easy way out, shirking their duty or blaming Rosie for their own omissions as, for example, in the case of the hostel staff whose only response to her recurrent harassment was to record the incidents in a book or, after she was threatened with a knife, to give her a sleeping pill; the social worker who said she was unable to help Rosie with her community charge summons; the community nurse who did not want to know about the problems Rosie was having with Beth; the unit manager who said it was not her job to handle complaints; the staff who managed Rosie's diet and then censured her for losing too much weight.

- *Arbitrary and repressive treatment*: Rosie has experienced a great deal of ill-natured behaviour on the part of staff aimed primarily at asserting their own authority. Examples include the refusal of workers to allow her to use the office phone, even though Rosie was willing to pay for her calls and the officer in charge and her deputy had given their permission; the threat by a keyworker to report Rosie to the police for objecting to sharing a double bed with another woman on holiday; the verbal bullying of the community nurse; the trouble she brings on herself by visiting the hospital without staff permission; being reduced to tears by staff at the social education centre for refusing to do the ironing as instructed; being told off for buying an ornament with her own money without first seeking staff approval. Although keen to avoid making trouble for herself, Rosie feels compelled to challenge rules or behaviour that she perceives as unreasonable. Her relations with staff express this contest between their efforts to exert control and her assertiveness.

- *Lack of personal respect and regard*: as her story shows, Rosie is easily wounded by behaviour that she sees as discourteous, belittling or designed to put her down. She was upset that Community Nurse Brightside failed to turn up at her birthday party or reply to her invitation, and that Community Nurse Sharpe never brought her baby for Rosie to see. She felt humiliated when the psychiatrist probed about the cleanliness of her house. She complained about staff discussing her personal affairs in public places, missing appointments, reading her letters, shouting at her and laughing behind her back. She objected to being made to see a male doctor, to her psychiatrist communicating with the hostel staff rather than directly with her and to having to use a public phone box at night without regard for her personal safety. For the most part, Rosie's relationships with practitioners are of a non-reciprocal kind in which she is expected to show but is not accorded respect, to listen without answering back, and to defer without question.

- *Lack of independent representation*: Even though Rosie knows her own mind, it is clear she has difficulties in getting practitioners to listen to her or take notice of what she says. Her problem is not lack of ability but lack of status. Practitioners, from young, part-time care assistants to hospital consultants, assume the right to tell her what to do. People like Rosie have need of access to independent advocates who would empower them, confront their devalued status, challenge bad practice and help them look after their own interests. Accountability also calls for an accessible and easy-to-understand complaints procedure such as the law now requires but few have yet devised.

These aspects of Rosie Spencer's experience of the services are not unique to her case but are more properly seen as structural features of the relationship between parents with learning difficulties and the service system. The two do not easily meld. Should parents come under services for families and children or services for people with learning difficulties? Specialist services tend to overlook their ordinariness. Generic services tend to overplay their learning difficulties. Practitioners have still much to learn about finding a balance between the autonomy parenting demands and the compliance the services exact.

Practice pointer 12: Practitioners must be aware of their capacity for exacerbating the stress on families and augmenting the problems they face.

Practice pointer 13: Practitioners must seek to avoid seeing parents only through the distorting mirror of existing services.

Practice pointer 14: The attitude of practitioners towards parents is as important as their actions; how support is delivered matters as much as what support is delivered.

Rosie Spencer's story as a topic

The life story approach produces data in the form of narrative rather than numbers. As Denzin (1989) says, 'lives are available to us only in words'. The process by which accounts of lives are produced and turned into text is therefore an important methodological issue in this kind of research with implications for the ownership and authenticity of the story as told. In this section, we take stock of the key challenges and compromises we encountered in compiling Rosie Spencer's story, as presented in the previous chapter, and the lessons they pose for research.

Rosie Spencer's story is the work of several authors: Rosie and Charlie as narrators, and the researchers as writers and editors. The first draft – pulling together interview transcripts, field reports and observations, notes of telephone conversations and other documentary material such as letters – was almost three times the length of Chapter 7. Even while still in the field, a researcher 'can never forget that there is much more to the "story" than he or she is getting' (Faraday and Plummer 1979). So it was with Rosie. But above and beyond this material never retrieved or uncovered, there is the additional loss from the process of selection involved in the preparation of the text as published.

Editing the raw material from the interviews and other sources was governed by two ideals or maxims: honesty (to the data, to Rosie as the subject and to our relationship) and readability. Our approach was to regard the researcher (as storyteller) as a writer under oath. Most expurgated material fell into one or more of the following categories of data: repetitions (an inevitable feature of extended interviewing but also a device Rosie used to signal her preoccupations, to avoid answering or to side-step a question she did not understand); expendable trivia that did not carry the story forward or add to our understanding of Rosie's world; excess detail (over and above that needed to convey the point); self-registering material (referring more to the researcher than the subject); and conversational packaging. In abridging the original draft to a manageable length, however, we are left with the feeling of having also rendered down Rosie Spencer's personality. Gone is some of her humour, her wit, her generosity, her lovable eccentricities, her sunny side – indeed, many of the traits that have brought her a lot of friends and kept the researchers in touch with her after the fieldwork ended. When all the pleasantries are removed, the chit-chat about Pooch the puppy and Flip the cat, the tale of Charlie's quarrel at the club or Beth's new job or Paul's holiday, the sharing of news and gossip, and all the other stuff of which the interviews were made, the edited narrative inevitably portrays Rosie in a narrow light. Researchers should harbour no illusions about the fact that the life story approach always betrays its subjects by representing them. At the same time, it leaves one pondering how much more is lost by research that fails to engage with the person at all.

Editing also involves a process of interpretation. Plummer (1983) draws a contrast between the researcher's and the subject's frame of reference and points out that the key issue in compiling life stories is the weight given to these respective viewpoints when selecting the material to include or exclude.

The form of Rosie Spencer's story is shaped by the fact of her having learning difficulties. She tended not to speak in long, uninterrupted stretches of narrative. Questions frequently elicited one-word or a simple phrase in reply. Information had often to be gleaned by direct rather than open-ended questioning. She was better able to handle questions about people and places than to cope with abstract ideas or make comparisons. She talked more easily about things happening in the here-and-now than about former times or past experiences. Also, as Biklen and Moseley (1988) found, observation is an important part of the interviewing process with people with learning difficulties. Rosie's feelings and concerns were more often revealed in her behaviour and her reaction to events and situations than through reflection and analysis.

All these factors played a part in deciding how the story should be told. There was insufficient continuous narrative to present the story entirely in Rosie's own words and to have loaned her the vocabulary she lacked would have given a false impression of her lucidity. Charlie was interviewed to provide some of the family background that could only be obtained by asking open-ended questions of the kind Rosie evaded. Her present-orientation meant that attention had to be given to what was going on in her life during the course of the fieldwork. This focus led, in turn, to a story structure that reflected the chronology of events as they occurred. Finally, the researcher's own voice is used to report material not available in the form of first-person narrative.

Rosie's story is properly seen, therefore, as the end-product of a collaborative process involving the pooling of knowledge and resources (especially time). This raises the issue of its ownership: whose story is it? Plummer (1983) highlights the continuum between life stories that are the property of their subjects (like diaries and autobiographies) and those that are the property of the researcher (where the third person interpretation of the original material prevails, as in Freud's case studies). Locating Rosie's story on this continuum is not easy. On the one hand, it is unlikely that Rosie would give the same prominence to her relationship with the researcher in recounting the same period in her life to a third party. In other words, another amanuensis would produce another story. On the other hand, it is not the researcher's story. No attempt has been made to impose a framework of analysis, the style is straight reportage, and the researcher's side of the story is omitted. On balance, the story probably falls somewhere towards the middle of Plummer's continuum as an account of what went on between Rosie and the researcher which deliberately suppresses the person of the researcher so as better to apprehend Rosie's world.

In order to check out the view that ownership of the story should best be regarded as shared (rather than, for instance, lost or stolen), it was read through to Rosie – excepting the extracts from the interview with Charlie – and the session recorded on tape. Nothing was added or subtracted as a result of her comments. We are satisfied that the version in this book has her full approval.

The issue of ownership is closely related to the problem of implicit or a priori conceptualization in doing life histories (Allport 1947). This refers to the danger of researchers subjugating the interpretation of their raw material to fit their own preconceived ideas or suppositions: of finding what they are looking for. Even going through the text with Rosie offers only a limited check against this sort of bias for she could be said to have verified merely what was in rather than what had been left out of the account. For this reason it is important to emphasize the distinction between 'the story' and 'the truth'. As Bowker (1993) has said, 'no faithful method of retrieving biographical "truth" exists'. Rosie Spencer's story is only one among many potential versions. Other people in her life would render different accounts. The most we can claim for the one published here is that it is true to the relationship from which it springs. As such it serves its purpose of making visible the social relations in which Rosie Spencer is embedded as a parent with learning difficulties and showing how she internalizes them as part of her own sense of self (Bertaux-Wiame 1981).

Most research on parents with learning difficulties draws on professionals for information. By giving the parents a voice, the life story approach gives them a chance to be heard publicly and so to reclaim their own lives. This has led some writers to suggest that researchers are almost invariably thrust into the role of advocate (Faraday and Plummer 1979; Bertaux and Kohli 1984) – a possibility which underlines the dangers of implicit conceptualization or blindness to their own motives. Certainly, as Bowker (1993) points out, 'establishing "acceptable" versions of lives is as much a political struggle for unknowns as it is for the famous'. The real point at issue, however, is the current status of our knowledge about parents with learning difficulties. As we have shown elsewhere in this book (see especially Chapter 4), the professionals who write the records and decide what to put in the files are themselves not immune to the criticism of implicit conceptualization. The only way of checking out the reliability of these official sources – and the part professionals themselves and their agencies play in people's lives – is by comparison with independent sources of biographical data. The preparation of Rosie Spencer's story emphasizes the importance of not taking professional judgements at face value. Prior to contacting the family we were warned by a social worker that Charlie Spencer was known to be a violent man. This reputation was based on the children having been physically abused and Rosie also having been knocked about. In the course of the research both of these incidents were denied by the victims themselves and other plausible explanations given. Rosie, for instance, said the doctor had presumed bruising on her arm had been inflicted by Charlie and she had not dared to contradict him. Once earned, however, Charlie's reputation had been passed on from worker to worker over a period of more than 15 years.

Berger (1966) has argued that biographies are not fixed in the past but subject to constant revision. Narratives always contain what Kohli (1981) has called a 'reconstructive element' in that past events are continually being reinterpreted in relation to the present. From this point of view, the past is malleable and flexible and changes in accordance with people's present situation and their ideas of what matters to them. There is another sense, too, in which biographies are always stories waiting to be told. Lives move on. Rosie Spencer is a case in point. Shortly after the fieldwork ended, Rosie complained that she had been sexually assaulted by a taxi driver regularly used by the hostel ('He was forcing me to have sexual intercourse with him. He told me not to tell anyone or he'd be in trouble'). Hostel staff responded angrily to her complaint. The taxi driver, they said, was 'respected' and 'trustworthy' and had been used by staff and residents for many years without any hint of misdoing. As a grandmother, she was old enough to know what's what: why was she making a fuss? A senior staff member flatly rejected her complaint, saying he had never tried anything with her. Although Rosie later reported bleeding and stomach pains, she was not taken to see her own doctor for over three weeks, by which time it was too late to press the case further. The hostel has continued using the same taxi driver (with the Department's official blessing), arguing that nothing improper has been reported by other residents, who wish to continue using his services, and who should be encouraged to make their own choices in such matters of daily living. Shortly afterwards, Rosie at last moved into her own flat as she had wanted (an event celebrated, of course, by a housewarming party attended by family and friends). Hers is still a closely knit family. Rosie is awaiting the arrival of her third grandchild: Paul and Sally's first baby. She still visits them every Saturday. Now that Paul has seen her flat, he has come to terms with the idea of his mother living alone. Beth drops round several times a week and cooks her a dinner on Sunday. They are saving up to go on holiday together. Charlie calls in now and again, unlike when she lived in the hostel, and they see each other most weekends at the club. Staff remain a persistent source of aggravation in her life. As she says: 'I'm still under hostel staff. I still don't feel my own boss. I says to officer in charge, if I'm out in community why have I to have the same staff and go shopping with same people from up at hostel? She says I have. Officer in charge!' She feels so powerless in the face of official harassment that she is refusing to take her medication for high blood pressure – even though she knows it will make her ill. Staff have warned she will bring trouble on herself if she talks about them to her psychiatrist (the keyworker who accompanied her on her last appointment relayed to the officer-in-charge what she had been saying). Now that she is no longer under the hostel GP, staff have also told her not to say anything about the incident with the taxi driver to her new doctor. On a brighter note, she likes her new community nurse who has agreed that Beth and Paul can go along with her to see the psychiatrist ('She said it's my appointment and I can choose who goes'). Rosie has still not seen Community Nurse Sharpe's baby. The last time they met she promised to send a photo. Rosie is waiting.

CHAPTER 9

Breaking up, breaking down

Child care law is about balancing the right of parents to bring up their children against the need to protect children from harm (Hayes 1993). Ever since Maria Colwell, the emphasis within the social work services has shifted more and more from supporting families to protecting children. The effect, as Prosser (1992) has observed, is that professional practice too often 'seems to see the good of the child requiring the sacrifice of the family'. Parents with learning difficulties are especially at risk of such a priori judgements because of ingrained doubts about their capacity for good-enough parenting summed up in the widespread presumption of incompetence. This outlook draws practitioners into making premature assessments of parenting failure that owe more to their own fears and prejudices than to the behaviour of the parents. Consequently, parents with learning difficulties continue to suffer the heartache and grief of having their children taken away because the lessons from research have not yet found their way into practice. The uphill struggle they face in proving their fitness for parenthood was examined in Chapter 4.

Child care law is also about what happens to children once they have been taken into care. Current legislation puts a high value on the principle of preserving family ties between children in care and their parents. However, the law only provides a broad framework within which decisions must be made. As Harris (1990) remarks, the 'day-to-day common sense interpretations of the experts and their managers will therefore shape the nature of child protection practice more than the subtleties of the language of jurisprudence'. Practitioners' views of what is best for the child will depend, among other things, on their assessment of the fitness of the parents. In the case of parents with learning difficulties, the value that practitioners place on their parental role may depend in part on how they value them as people. Where the parents are seen as having little or no positive contribution to make to the child's upbringing, they may conclude that the preservation of contact is not in the child's welfare. The dangers of causing avoidable suffering and trauma to parents and children alike by failing to appreciate the nature of the bonds within the family and the capacity of the parents for love and affection (Galliher 1973) are all too real.

Fourteen of the 20 families in our study had one or more of their children placed in care at some time or other. In two cases the child was admitted on a short-term placement and rehabilitated with the family soon afterwards. In the other 12 families, the children were either removed permanently (16) or remained in care for periods of between nine months and six years (4). Among those taken into permanent care, eight were removed at birth or when only a matter of a few months old and the rest were taken sometime between the ages of one and seven years. Overall, then, the majority of the parents had suffered the torment of losing a child: like Ms Austin, who said of her first baby, removed at birth ten years ago, 'I still miss him', or Ms Burnley, whose first child was taken at two weeks old, and who now says, 'I'm just waiting. I'm going to wait till he knocks on the door. You see, if I have him back I'll be a family, a proper family.' Gloria Gore's three children have all been taken into care. Her sister knows the hurt doesn't heal: 'Gloria cries but she doesn't cry in front of people; she goes upstairs. She feels lost without them. She keeps saying she's no life. She wishes she were dead.' Mr Hardy, whose first child had been fostered and later adopted, spoke for many others when he said: 'Since that day he went our lives is not the same. We want us own children in us own home. But Social Services, once they've got their teeth in, they won't let go. We wanted our children and we love our children. We want to be a family. I mean that's what you get married for, to have a family and look after them and that. I thought to myself, if they take your child they might as well take me an' all. We're not complete. It's in my mind: never let go till that lad walks through that front door. I shall be there.'

Sarah and Geoff Armstrong belong to this group of parents. Six months before the study started, their eldest child, Mark, had been fostered with Geoff's brother. When we first met them their two other children, Carl and Kate, were still at home. During the course of the research, both were also taken away. Our interviews with the Armstrongs thus provide an insight into the impact of events on the family as seen through the eyes of the parents themselves and reflected in their feelings at the time. The purpose in presenting the Armstrongs' story at length is not to question the rights and wrongs of the decision to remove the children. But their case does raise wider issues about the handling of such decisions and the way they are carried out that have a bearing on parents with learning difficulties in general.

We have no personal accounts by parents with learning difficulties of losing their children. These decisions are invariably presented from a professional perspective with the professional's voice coming over loudest. The effect has been to highlight the inadequacies of parents at the expense of their ordinary human feelings. The danger of seeing the problems and not the people is that, in seeking to safeguard the child, unnecessary harm and personal suffering may be caused to the parents and the wider family. The Armstrongs' story portrays this danger as a living reality, one sadly shared with many other parents in the study.

Sarah Armstrong says what other mothers felt. She talks more than her husband because Geoff, mindful that we had been introduced via their social worker and initially suspicious of our motives, refused at first to allow any recording or notetaking. Although he gave a different slant to his own behaviour, they shared the same view of what was happening to them under the pressure of events. The fact that they were experiencing in the here-and-now the forced break-up of their family gives power and immediacy to the narrative. Their story obliges anyone who holds doubts about the capacity of parents with learning difficulties to love, to think again. Other parents who suffered the same loss experienced the same sort of trauma but either lacked the words to provide a sustained account of how they felt at the time or found thinking about it too painful (Kathy Gordon, whose child was just coming up for adoption, was unable to speak about it at all over the course of four interviews). The Armstrongs' story stands by itself as a source of understanding. We shall resist the temptation to analyse and reflect on its wider significance. Our position, as Bogdan and Taylor (1976) remark, 'is that at times and to a much greater extent than we do now, we must listen to people who have been labelled . . . with the idea of finding out about ourselves, our society, and the nature of the label'.

The Armstrongs' story

Sarah and Geoff used to live next door to each other on a large council estate. Sarah enjoyed a happy childhood. After leaving special school, she attended an adult training centre, doing voluntary work in an old people's home, until she married. Geoff remembers very little about his childhood: 'I only know what my sister tells me.' When he was five, he was involved in a road accident and sustained severe head injuries. For many years he was unable to speak at all. He attended a special residential school into his teens, going home only for holidays. The regime was tough, punishment frequent and brutal, and he was glad finally to be transferred to a special school near his home. He lived at home with his mother until she died when he was 30. It took him a long time to get over her death, and during this period his sister had kept an eye on him. Four years later he married Sarah.

Both Sarah and Geoff have learning difficulties. Sarah has good literacy skills although she admits to being 'terrible at reckoning up': 'I just get the shopping in the basket and hope for the best at till, hoping I've got enough to pay for it.' Geoff is still learning to read and write, but has no problems with arithmetic. He does acknowledge a 'weakness for the horses' that has led them into debt in the past. For the moment, though, money is not one of their worries.

For the last five years, Geoff has worked as a council road sweeper. The hours are long and the work is hard. Sarah gets him up at 5.30 a.m. and makes his snap. He leaves the house at 6.00 a.m., returning home again just after 6.00 p.m. He gets a half-hour break at midday for lunch. At weekends he busies himself in the garden, growing vegetables for the family and tending the flower beds. Sarah complains that his mother spoilt him: 'She used to want to do everything for him and now he expects it from me, and I've told him I'm not going to be his slave. He's got to help as much as I do.'

It is February. Our first meeting. Six months ago the Armstrongs' eldest child, Mark, who's almost seven, had been fostered with Geoff's brother. Their other two children, Carl, aged three, and Kate, two, are still at home. A court case is pending to decide the future of all three children. Toys cover the floor of their neat and tidy council house. With her little girl curled up next to her on the settee, Sarah talks:

'I've had social workers from children being babies. Mark's been everywhere from being a little lad and then he was put in hospital for 28 days cos his dad had hit him. He went into care, then he's been home, then he's been into care again. It's been like that all the time. Mark burnt the bedspread on the mattress, he's set fires in the quarries, he went with older boys near the railway on this tourer bike. But I don't actually think that he's done it on his own. The other kids have provoked him to do it, I think. We see him every Wednesday, just for an hour.'

'He's quietened down now. Talking to him, you wouldn't think butter would melt in his mouth. I just wish I could've done for Mark as my family's done. I couldn't cope with Mark. He's too much and I feel bad about it.'

'When Geoff hit Mark he went on probation for two years. He never hit them again after that, never hit them again.'

'My husband Geoff had an accident when he was five and when he gets these attacks his temper goes. He doesn't pronounce his words properly. But I think that's because he had a car accident so it's brought him a twisted brain.'

'He were in a boarding school because, when he were young, he couldn't talk or anything. So now he goes to hospital on a Wednesday and he has speech therapy lessons, like lessons to learn him to read and write – what he's

missed out he's learning now from his childhood. I mean I'm not a good
scholar but I'm brighter than my husband.'

'Sometimes it's 20 past six when Geoff gets in. The kids are generally ready
for bed by the time he comes home. They're in bed between quarter to seven
and seven o'clock. Carl gets up when his dad's up in a morning. He's up for
day then. Geoff's out of here at six o'clock. I mean, that's pretty early.'

'We have problems with Carl now, plays me up terrible. I've had to move
my cabinet upstairs because he smashed my ornaments. So I mean, he is hard
work. These last week or two he's been very hard work. Carl and Kate go to
my family's on a weekend. My brother has Kate and my sister has Carl, so it
eases off a bit. Carl's in day care three times a week – Mondays, Wednesdays
and Fridays.'

'At the moment my family's put in for two children. If things happen when
we go to court, if they have to go into care the other two, they will go to my
family's if the judge says so. Then I only see them once a week. Which I don't
want to lose them. I want to be a mother what could look after her children.
My solicitor says, do you feel that you can cope with your children on your
own without your husband. I says, well, I can't really say because I haven't
been on my own.'

'Social workers come in and have a talk to me, ask how Carl's been, and I
tell them if he's doing wrong. I mean I'm not allowed to smack them, so I've
got to find a way to discipline him. I haven't to smack him because of Mark
having marks when he was a child. She doesn't stop all that long and they ask
me how Geoff's been with them. I mean last night I stopped him from hitting
Carl. He was playing up, he wouldn't give up and he was getting his dad
worked up. I'd rather deal with him than Geoff because he seems to make
them stand and hold their shoulders and Carl's saying he's hurting him,
which he doesn't realize he's hurting him and he doesn't mean to do it, it's
just the way he disciplines them.'

'If he's in a mood, I get the kids ready and go for a walk somewhere. I go to
my mam. I say look mam, I don't think I'll be able to cope with Geoff if the
kids go. I have thought about leaving him after it's all over but you can't
really blame Geoff for what's happening with kids. But I can when he hit
Mark when he was young. I feel now that I should have left him when it
happened.'

'We see Mark from half past three while half past four. We've tried to get
more access* but we can't have it because social workers have to be there to
assess him. We had Mark on his own once and social workers thought that
we'd put words into Mark because he was wanting to come home. He said he
couldn't be with his auntie and uncle for 12 years and we just sat cuddling
him, you see. I mean it's upsetting when you go, but Geoff's feeling it now

---

* The events recounted in this chapter took place during the period in which the
implementation of the 1989 Children Act brought a change in legal terminology . For
example, access is now referred to as 'contact', and custody is now termed 'residence'. At
the time of our study, these changes had not seeped through into the everyday parlance
of either workers or their clients.

and I think that's why he's getting more uptight with social workers because he's feeling it more. We saw him without Social Services at Christmas because it was a family party. We had that to ourselves so it was a relief then.'

'Kate's well mannered, you know. She's talkative. Boys are more mischievous, boisterous than what girls are. Mark were always Geoff's favourite. He would take Carl out, but he said he didn't feel the same way. Carl mocks him. He copies when his dad tries to tell him off. Carl's too active.'

Two weeks later. Sarah is still in her dressing gown at lunch time. The other two children had been taken into temporary care the previous week. Kate is with Sarah's brother and Carl with Sarah's sister.

'I don't bother with neighbours. I used to go with Carol next door to playgroup on a Thursday with kids. But since Carl and Kate've been away I've not been nowhere. I get that fear. I don't want to go out. I don't want to see anybody . . .'

'. . . All I know is that Social Services want the other two together. That's all I know. Because, the thing is, they think that Carl will get like Mark because he's following in his footsteps. He's like Mark in some ways, but in other ways he isn't. What it is, me and Geoff can't protect them from everyday risks. They've got that against us as well. But it will be up to the courts. If the judge feels they're at risk, he'll let them go. I've got to work really hard next week to fight for them. You see there's a lot of people sitting in court an' all. There's your barrister, your solicitor, you've got Social Services' solicitor, their barrister, you've got the official solicitor from London, and you got a doctor doing reports on you. I mean you've got a lot of people to answer questions to. And it really is a bit much in court.'

'I just wish we could be a normal family and not have anything to do with Social Services. The problem I've got is, when I'm talking to somebody and kids are round the house, I've got to stand up and watch them at the same time. Where the social worker, when she came and the kids were here, she could tell what they were up to, where me I've got to listen. If I'm talking to someone, I have to listen careful cos my mind's not properly there in every way. And I find that difficult, me.'

'My sister-in-law wants Mark to stay with her because he's settled there and the solicitor felt that if we fight for Mark it'll cause problems. So me and Geoff agreed for him to stay there but to fight for other two. I mean you can go on fighting for ever but you'll not get them back. They think the other two'll grow up like Mark. I said to my solicitor, you cannot say now if Kate or Carl will be like Mark.'

'The social worker calls to see how we are. She'll ask how Carl is and I'll tell her what he's been doing. She advises me what to do. If he's naughty, I either send him upstairs to his bedroom or I make him sit down. People say you shouldn't bribe him with sweets but, if they're not going to behave, you've got to do something. I mean, I can't smack him so he's got to be punished some way, so I says you can't have sweets until you behave yourself. That's what my mam used to do with us, so why shouldn't I do it?'

April. Sarah and Geoff have lost custody of all three children. Before the hearing, their solicitor (who had been recommended to them by Social Services) had warned the ruling would more than likely go against them. The social worker said in court that the children had not been neglected but were not fed regularly: she had only seen them eat cakes and biscuits and couldn't detect any cooking smells on her visits. She had also seen Sarah take Kate out on a cold day in dress, coat, socks and shoes but no hat and gloves. The judge ruled that Sarah and Geoff's families keep the children. All three are now living with different relatives. Sarah and Geoff are allowed to see them for one hour a week and only when social workers are present. They have been told by Social Services that they are 'slow' and that they have a 'disability problem'.

'The judge said we were good parents, we just couldn't cope. I feel they're somebody else's children. I know they're my kids but going somewhere else to see them is so strange. I feel strange, too. The kids are calling their dad 'Geoff', and he gets angry and upset. If I ask for anything for my kids in front of them, like asking for Mark to attend a party, we have been told it would go against our access. So when we see them we feel we can't say anything. The last time we saw Carl he asked if his house was still in Elm Street.'

Two months on. Sarah has taken an overdose after becoming severely depressed. Geoff, too, has been under a lot of stress. He'd struck Sarah during an argument about money and she'd left him for a month to live with a distant relative. He'd bought her flowers and asked her to come home. They were now back together again. They've been told their daughter has a heart murmur and that she has to wear glasses. Both are still very down . . .

'I were really low and I just went for tablets. I went to see my doctor and he said you and your husband have got to pull yourself together. Told him about the court case and everything. He said whenever you're feeling low and not looking after yourself they think that you're not capable of looking after your children. That's the way the doctor put it. But, as I said to him, you don't know what pressure is really like, you don't know what depression is. I mean I could have gone for him. I just broke down, I was crying. I tell you, I took all bottle. I'll tell you summat, I'd never do it again. Oh, I were awful. I'm not taking them now. I take my nerve tablets. I take one in morning and one at night time. I can't do without them. He won't let me have any more after this course because he says I get too addicted to tablets. So he won't let me have no more. I've always suffered with me nerves. I've always been on tablets part of my life. I come off them now and then, but if I'm under pressure . . . Some days I get where I want to take overdoses and end my life. When I'm in town I'm going to see if I can talk to somebody. I'm going to go to Samaritans. It might help because I'd end up doing summat if I don't talk to nobody. Can't sleep. I went to bed at half past one this morning and I still wakened at half past four. I feel tired but yet I don't sleep.'

'Now Geoff's back at work he's coming round a bit. But I think it were due to him being off work. He's worse when he's in house, gets more ratty. He wouldn't get dressed in a morning for work. I used to have to make him get ready. He'd sit and sit till it were time to bloody rush about. At one stage, he got me putting his socks on. He were getting that way where he couldn't be bothered to do anything because he got so low. I'm off to town today after dinner to meet Geoff on that half past four bus. He wants me to meet him and come home with him.'

'He gets upset when he's seen kids. Because he gets so worked up, and it's uncomfortable when you go and see them because I'm irritable when I go. If Geoff's upset, it makes me worse. And I just go, I just sit there quiet then, till I get it out of me. But Geoff was saying last week that Carl's changing. He's not the same person is Carl. His mind's in another world. Like when he first went away he'd come for a cuddle, but now you've to go to him for a cuddle. You see, you can't say nowt in front of kids because they write it down. You've got to be very careful.'

'I told Geoff if we're going to be back together we've got to make a go of it, if not then we might as well get divorced. But I know I wouldn't get custody of kids because they'll never be back. They'll never be back while they're 18. Geoff can't get it through to him that they're not coming back. I can't do with him at home, oh I can't, I've got to go out. I can't do with him keep on nagging about kids coming home.'

'I've been on day trips with him and I've been on holiday with him and it's awful without kids. Because we go to places where we've took the kids, and I want to be home. I see kids in my mind. I just want to be home away from other kids.'

'I've had letters and that for Carl to start school so I gave them to social worker to tell them that he's not here. I was going to do it myself but Geoff said it was too embarrassing for me. But you've got to face up to it, think about what you're going to say. You have to do it.'

'We don't see our families very often. I think they've been about once since kids have been away. See, when they come, they can't bring kids. One of them has to look after them while they come and see us. Our families must never bring the kids round this area in case we bump into each other. Geoff asked the social worker what would happen if we met them accidentally in town. She said it would be OK, but we must not plan to meet them. Like, other night, I went to see my mam and I'd to go home because kids were going to see my mam. You see, if kids are there, I have to come out, me. So I went before kids come. I says, oh, I'll have to go mam, give them a kiss and then I went. But she must have felt it, my mam.'

'Once I got Carl a pair of trainers and it never dawned on me that I had to make arrangements with kids being there. I didn't think it'd make any difference. But because I'd made arrangements on the phone to meet my sister, Social Services got on to it, didn't they. I didn't do it to meet Carl. I did it to meet my sister, so I could give her trainers. But, after that, I couldn't phone my family then. I just see kids on a Wednesday. I would like a list of what I can and what I can't do, me.'

'I mean Carl's saying now that his dad's put him away. Now if he can be like that all time, he's going to grow up thinking it. Young people have turned against their parents, won't have nowt to do with them whatsoever. And I feel it for them. I don't want to go through the same way as what them people are going through because they're in a shocking state. I just hope to God it never happens to me. Today Kate were close to me. She put her arms round me and I said no, I said, I'm sorry love I'll have to go. She cried her heart out. Carl thought he were coming home. He just stood and watched us go, as if he were wondering why we were going.'

'My brother is getting married some time in September. But I don't know if we'll be able to go to the wedding because kids'll be there. But I'll feel it if we don't go, I would. I cried when we went to kids' party. The social worker said this is a one-off. I cried and all they said was, if you come and upset the kids you'll not see them again. It's alright for them to say hold it back, don't cry in front of kids. I couldn't help it.'

'Geoff thinks some day that kids are going to come home and he thinks that kids are going to spend a weekend with us. But that'll never happen, I know that. So I don't say much to him because it'll set him off, so I keep my peace. They've told me they're not coming home while they're 18. I believe them. You see, if I got pregnant now, that'd be taken into care as well. They wouldn't let me keep it. I said to Geoff, I says, I feel like living at Australia away from it all. But there again, kids is over here. He wouldn't move because of kids. I feel now that there's nothing over here for us. Family doesn't see me much, his family doesn't bother with Geoff, so what's the point in staying over here?'

One week later and the start of the school holidays. As Sarah talks, the voices of children playing outside filter through the open window.

'Before we went to court, the solicitor who we have, he always said that Social Services would get my kids and it happened. So I accepted what he said. What could I do, I couldn't do anything. Oh, I just love Wednesdays to come and I can see my kids. It really is lovely when they put their arms round you.'

'I find it really hard being here and he's at work and there's nobody to talk to. When I've got my work done, you're just looking at four walls. And when I'm in house, I get depression.'

'My sister-in-law's off on holiday at the moment. She's having a break from Mark. He's stopping with another couple. Last Sunday, Carl went to

Whitby and he showed me photos and it were good. But Geoff feels very hurt over Carl because, I mean, he loves him and he cuddles his dad but Geoff feels hurt in another way. Carl told his dad that his dad's put him away. So I spoke to social worker about it and she doesn't think that Carl's got a mind to say that. But I mean, he's four. If you say owt to social workers, they say Geoff's imagining it. I don't understand it at all, me. The social workers just say it's because we're not educational – that's nowt to go by.'

'Some days it's very hard to live with Geoff and other days he'll be all right. Like last night, I were going to leave him because he wouldn't shut up on about the kids. So I got up, I said, if you don't shut up I'm going and I won't come back. And he's carrying on, stopping me at door saying he doesn't want me to leave and I said, well, buck your ideas up then.'

'I was talking to the headmistress about the kids yesterday. She said, "It turned out for the best, didn't it?" I said, maybe you think it did. She said, because Mark was hard work for you. I says, yes, but I wouldn't say it turned out for the best.'

'It's good that we can see them every week now but if Geoff carries on he'll spoil the access and I won't be able to go and see them then. They think that if we have more access to kids, the kids are going to be more upset. We've to be very careful. I mean, when we're at access, they're watching what we're doing and what we say. It really is a nightmare. We've been told by the social workers not to bring them sweets every week because they'll expect it every week. They didn't ever say in court that they're away while they're 18. But the Social Services have said that that's what the court order means – while they're 18.'

'They are taking our kids away that we have brought on to this earth. I thought you had to have some evidence before your kids were removed.'

October. Sarah had spent two days the previous week looking after her little nephew while his mother went to work. Today she is busy washing and is going to the job centre in the afternoon. Geoff has been in hospital recently with phlebitis. Sarah makes a cup of coffee . . .

'The last access we went Geoff was upset. So the social worker took him outside, you know, away from kids so that they wouldn't see him being upset. The solicitor spoke to him to tell him to keep calm – because they could stop his access you see. Geoff doesn't like Carl calling him Geoff. He talks to me about it and I say, look Geoff, it is confusing for Carl. Carl doesn't understand. He calls my sister 'Mummy', and me 'Mammy Sarah'. I just laugh it off. I know I shouldn't but what can you do? I mean I've accepted the way it is, but Geoff cannot. This time it's going to be the worse Christmas I've ever had because we won't have kids. When I come home I cry. It doesn't bother me seeing kids on access but when I come home, that's when I start. Or if I'm in house on my own I sit and roar. You've just got to grin and bear it. These photos, I mean them there, I don't look at them. That's our Kate. She wears glasses now, can you see them? She's altered since she's been away.'

'The doctor's been on three occasions to see how we go on with kids and how they respond to us. She keeps an eye on Carl because they say my sister's having a few problems with him. When Geoff got upset on access it caused Carl to wet bed. You see kids feel it an all, so doctor says be very calm on the access.'

'Mark's been away for a long time. He talks to us. He has a cuddle but he's getting that age where he gets embarrassed, you know what I mean? He doesn't seem to like it. But he still loves us.'

'I'm having a lot of headaches. I've been to doctor's. I'm on that injection every three month. I couldn't take that pill – that were giving me headache – so they give me that injection. I'm frightened of getting pregnant because they'll take it off me. I can sleep all afternoon and still have headache when I wake up. I keep going to doctor's and he said I can't do anything more for you. He says you're going to have to learn to cope with it, but it drives me mad. Many times I bang my head on that wall because it really is awful. I get it down here and across your eyes and my eyes hurt, my nose aches. I were going crazy on biscuits for last few weeks because I'm bored. I've put more weight on now but I'm going to have to give up. It's bad when you get older.'

'My mam's been on about seeing our Mark and I say, "Look mam, if I ask for owt it makes it worse because they could stop our access if we keep asking for things". Like Geoff, he wants to take them on a day trip and things, and if we keep asking for that they'll go to court and stop us access. So you can't ask for things.'

'You see, if they go to court and say they want to adopt the kids, we've got a right to fight against that. I wouldn't let the kids be adopted. I think my brother might try. He's close to Kate. If we have the kids home, he'd find it hard. He'd be in the same way as me and Geoff.'

'I'd have my kids at home but Geoff doesn't help me much with them, you know what I mean. That's why they went away – because I couldn't cope. Geoff used to leave me to do everything. He'd watch the telly. When I were cooking I had to keep coming in here and watching them at same time. It were hard work. If they had toys out he'd kick the toys away. I used to put them away to keep peace. They didn't have nowt to do then. They used to play up all time. He didn't help me much at home – he doesn't now. He thinks when he's been at work all day he's done enough. Now they're away he thinks that he should have done this, he should have done that with them. I say, well it's too late, Geoff.'

'If they came back, he'd help me for about three weeks and then he'd go to his old ways. When I come back after I left him he's all right for a couple of days then he kicked my door in, then he grabbed me by the bloody neck – tried to squeeze me to death. But I've told him, next time I won't stand for it because I'll knife him. I mean I shouldn't have to put up with that. When I nag him to do something he gets frustrated. He'll say, "You get on my bloody nerves". Like yesterday, I were getting him mad. I said, "Look Geoff, do summat". Because he sits for hours watching box. He'll have it loud and it does my head in.'

'Social Services could change over the years, the access could get less, what they've told Geoff. Social worker usually comes here to see how I am, how I cope with Geoff, keeps track of me. She came Monday, see how I went on with him on holiday. I thought it were a good holiday but he was bored. I enjoyed the caravan because I got away from Social Services because when you're on the access they're watching you all the time.'

'Saturday we bumped into Kate. She was in a push chair, and we were saying it'd be nice if we could just go over to market and get her a toy, but we couldn't do that. I did stop to talk to her, Kate, I can't ignore her, you know what I mean? If we did it regular, Social Services'd want to know what was up.'

'Geoff has said that he'd like Kate home for the weekend but solicitor thinks it's too early because they've only been away six months. I'd have coped with Kate. But Carl he was a handful and I feel ashamed of myself, I do, because I think now I made some mistakes. He's lots of energy has Carl. I mean he's on go all the time and he takes some settling down.'

'I wanted a flat for me and Geoff – put in for a flat with not having kids – but he says they're coming back home in ten years. I said, "Geoff, they're not". You see, I've got it through to me now that they're not coming home while they're 18. But he says things could change with kids.'

'I've got a friend on estate, I'm not kidding you, she lays on settee all time, settee and that's filthy. She has a social worker but they don't do nowt to take kids away and I don't think she should have kids. She's got one away what were glue sniffing and she's got other two. I can't understand why they let them keep their two children when the house is in a state. I mean it's absolutely filthy. I say that to Geoff anytime – why on earth are they letting people have their kids and mine is away? My house is clean. I said it doesn't stand to any reason.'

'I'm going to job centre and see what they've got. They haven't got one here. They used to have but they shut it down. It's a video shop now. You have to go to next town.'

A month later. The kitchen has been newly papered and the sitting room repainted twice.

'I have Prothiodin for me nerves and Diazepam for depression. It doesn't help me very much. I mean, I've got a part-time job now – a fortnight since – cleaning. Five while quarter past seven. It gives me a break away from him. Some days I can't stand being in house with him.'

'I got in touch with the counselling person. Well, social worker got in touch with her and she came to see me. She said, doesn't Geoff understand why they've been taken away? I said, he does but he can't cope with situation. She wanted to make arrangements to meet him. He says, I haven't time to meet her. He doesn't want to help himself.'

'He didn't play with them. Geoff's like this. When he's been to work all day he's tired, he wants his tea and he wants to sleep, that's Geoff. Now on access he hasn't played with them much . . . whether it's because Social Services are there watching him all the time. He's saying things to the kids. And not only that, Geoff's upsetting the foster parents. I feel it for them because when we've gone they have to cope with our kids. And it's not going to be easy for them, as it's not easy for us. But Geoff's not thinking about other people, he's just thinking of himself.'

'Our Carl doesn't bother with his dad much on the access. If Carl asks for anything, he'll ask my sister because he calls her mam. He says, "Mammy Sarah" or "Daddy Geoff". Well, Geoff doesn't like that. I mean it's so confusing for them kids. Kate calls my brother dad and calls our Julie her mam. If she asks me for summat I say, "Go ask your dad". I can't say "Ask your Auntie Julie". But Geoff slipped up. Kate must have wanted something and Geoff said, "Auntie Julie". Well, she started calling her Auntie Julie. But the Social Services didn't like it.'

'I think if social worker was here on her own with Geoff, I think he'd go for her because he's got it in for her. I mentioned it to her anyway. He would, because he's so annoyed with her. She knows, she knows all right. She came on Thursday, come up to talk to us. She knows I'm having this carry on with Geoff. I mean, when he gets upset I've got it to cope with when I come home. They haven't got it to cope with. They don't have to live with it.'

'This Wednesday there's a meeting. He said he's going to kick the table. I'll just walk out because I won't cope with it. I'm dreading it on Wednesday, I really am. Geoff's going to hear some nasty things what he won't like. I wish it were today instead of Wednesday – get it over with. It's to do with the access – they're cutting access down. Like once a fortnight or once a month or something. He'll blow his top, I know he will. If he's going to carry on, it's giving them chance – isn't it? – to do it. He's upsetting them every week. It's same routine every week. And it'll be worse for Geoff. He said that if they cut it down to a month, or once a fortnight, or have less time with them like half an hour, he said it's a waste of time. But I wouldn't say that because, even though it's half an hour, he'll see kids. But he's going to have to accept it at the end. There's nowt else you can do. And it's his own fault that he's carried on like this to make them cut the access down. He says he can't accept it, ever.'

'I said that, if he's going to carry on like this, I'll stop seeing my kids because it's not fair. If they're going to be distressed, how's the foster parents going to cope? I think of them, I don't think of myself, I think of them what's got kids. That's what's worrying me now with Geoff upsetting them. They could go in a home then – couldn't they? – if they're too distressed and they can't cope with them. But they seem to be coping well just now, even though Geoff's upsetting them. Because Kate's asking our Julie if she lives there, because she's so disturbed if you know what I mean.'

'When I'm fed up with myself, I'm in bed for eight. He likes Sky movies but I'm not one for television. I just sit about. If I'm bored I find summat to do in house. I can't sleep unless I take my tablet, I've got to have tablets. Geoff doesn't take any tablets. Doesn't like me taking them. During day I've got television on, but I can't be bothered with it. I just like it like this. I just sit here all day. I think about kids, what they'll be like when they're older. Geoff made me annoyed last night. He said when Kate gets older, if she started wanting to get married, and she asked my brother to give her away, and she didn't want her own dad to give her away, he said he wouldn't have owt to do with her. I says, well, that's wrong because she's your own flesh and blood. If you don't think owt of her if she's going to get married when she's older, you won't think of her now while she's young.'

It is the end of November and nobody answers the door. The garden shows signs of neglect and old newspapers have blown in off the street. Two days later the house is still empty. Sarah's neighbour hasn't seen her for a few days. Four days after this visit a letter arrives from Sarah:

I am writing to Say thank you for letting me know by letter that you had been to see me.

Sorry I was not at home because I have been doing Some extra hours at work because Some one at work came of Sick So I had do going in and Cover up and do their Job as well So its been very hard going this last week or So.

I took all my tablets last weekend. I was very poorly. I don't think I Can Carry on much more Coping with things any Longer. I go back to see my own doctor this Monday coming to see what he says.

I have bought some things for the three kids for Christmas. We had the meeting with the Social Services and my Family and geoff's Family came to the meeting. we all had our Say each One of us and about the Kids. how well they Said they look.

the Social Services have put Forward a little party For Kids me and geoff are going to be their which is on December 23rd. its going to be at their offices. we Saw the children last wednesday but they have put the Access for a monthly basses because (the social worker) Says that the Kids are getting stressed because the Say geoff was upseting them by Saying to Kids do you want to Come home thats the reason why they have changed the Access. I don't know how long this is going to last but they Say until next may. See how the Kids are.

I do find it very difficult to accept the monthly visits to see the Kids. I got are Carls First School photograph last Friday. I Can go to visit my Sister the one who as are Carl but I have to go before he Comes home From School.

I go down after one oclock while 3 oclock and then I go into town to Catch my bus For work.

I tried to give you a wring on the phone from where I live but the phone was not working. anyway have a good Christmas you your Husband and your Family.

happy Xmas and a very happy New Year.

Please Keep in touch with me. because theirs only you what understands what I am going through anyway good luck For now. S. Armstrong

Twelve months after their children were taken into care, Mr and Mrs Armstrong moved to a smaller council house in a village eight miles from their original home. They were sad to leave the area in which they had lived all their lives and keenly felt the distance between them and their families. Geoff was much closer to his place of work but Sarah no longer had a job and instead visited her mother most afternoons.

Sarah had recently been referred to the local hospital for a brain scan because of the severe and frequent headaches she suffered.

Geoff's brother and his wife, who take care of their elder boy, have themselves been concerned by the way the access arrangements are causing so much suffering for everybody. They are talking about approaching Social Services, or even going to court if necessary, with the suggestion that Geoff and Sarah be allowed to take Mark out for the day or have him stop over for a night at a weekend.

The foster families also have become nervous about social workers being around when visits take place and would much prefer there to be more freedom for family members to visit each other when they wanted without being watched all the time. At present Geoff and Sarah have to be very careful about when they visit any of their family in case the children are in the house. They have resigned themselves to the fact that the children will not come back to live with them, but they are hopeful that they might be allowed more time with them as the years go by. Geoff has the final word:

'I've no faith in God after what's happened. It's no good banking my hopes up. I've done it before and I've been disappointed. But I've seen it in my dreams. All five of us together.'

CHAPTER 10

Good practice guidelines

In this last chapter we draw together the lessons for good practice in working with parents with learning difficulties that have emerged from our review of the research literature and from our own study. Of course, good practice involves more than just a simple list of dos and don'ts. The skill comes in knowing when and how best to apply them. Good practice in working with parents who have had a child removed obviously calls for something different than good practice in supporting a couple with a new baby. Without reference to real problems or real cases, broad guidelines always have an abstract or even self-righteous quality. Our hope is that our text has provided the human foundation for these statements of principle.

Much remains to be learned in this field, not least about how to achieve a balance between the welfare of children and the rights of parents. The evidence of our research suggests that too often this balance is unfairly tipped against parents. Certainly we must be sure that all children are protected from abuse and neglect. In doing so, however, we must also ensure that parents are not themselves subjected to abuse by the system. Prosser (1992) has identified a number of defining characteristics of what he terms 'system abuse' based on parents' perceptions of their treatment at the hands of child protection agencies. These include actions that harm the people they are supposed to help; snap judgements taken on the basis of inadequate evidence; failing to involve people in decisions affecting them; adding to the problems already faced by families; seeing people in isolation from their close relationships; and treating individuals as ciphers. Most of the families in our study had met with some of these practices, a few had encountered them all. The guidelines set out below may serve as a corrective to the pressures within the system that otherwise easily lead to the victimization of parents with learning difficulties.

We suggested in Chapter 1 that a study of parenting would provide a new angle of vision on such important contemporary issues as normaliz-ation, 'ordinary life' ideas, community care, the rights and citizenship of people with learning difficulties, the notion of good parenting, and social justice and discrimination. As a way of winding up our study, by returning to where we began, we have used these headings as a framework for listing our good practice guidelines. We are finishing back at the beginning in another sense, too. These guidelines are no more than a starting point. A great deal of work remains to be done in the field of parenting by people with learning difficulties if the influence of prejudicial attitudes and misconceptions on policy and practice is to be eliminated. We should like to think our study has helped to lift the veil a little. Our hope is that it will encourage others to go further.

Normalization

- Accept responsibility for ensuring that parents are given the opportunity to acquire adequate child care skills and to learn appropriate parenting behaviour.
- Assessment, intervention and support must have regard to the function-ing of the family as a unit.
- Avoid seeing all the problems parents may be having entirely in terms of their learning difficulties.
- Avoid the mistake of assuming that parents with learning difficulties do not have the same feelings of care and affection for their children as other parents or that their family bonds are weaker.
- Respect for and support of the emotional bond between parent(s) and children should be the starting point for any intervention in the family.
- Be careful not to undermine the socially valued aspects of the parenting role.
- Be sensitive to the similarities between the parenting problems of people with learning difficulties and other at-risk families and respond in a like-minded way.
- Do not allow a partner without learning difficulties to have all the say; special efforts must be made to involve the parent with learning difficulties.
- Ensure parents are involved in decisions affecting their lives.
- Never underestimate people's capacity to change.
- Support should be provided to parents and children as people first.

'Ordinary Living'

- Affirm parents' identity as members of the community through the use of ordinary services and facilities.
- Avoid seeing the needs of parents only through the distorting lens of existing services.
- Be prepared to take a longer-term view of the family life cycle when making decisions.
- Beware the danger of segregated services leading to segregated needs.
- Do not overlook the emotional needs of the parents themselves.
- Service providers must be responsive to any informal support system already in place and ensure they do not interfere with its functioning.
- Services need to be organized in such a way that parents are made to feel competent, have a hand in solving their own problems and feel in control of events.
- Support is more effective when directed to the survival and maintenance needs of families, followed by child care tasks, than to modifying styles of interaction within the family.
- The maintenance and generalization of new learning is assisted by teaching in real-life settings rather than in the classroom or clinic, and by the involvement and support of fathers or partners.

Community Care

- Trainers themselves need to be experienced in working with people with learning difficulties.
- A positive relationship between trainer and parent is one of the most valuable curriculum resources.
- Advice and support tends to be more effective and carry more weight when tempered by first-hand experience of parenting.
- Be prepared to show patience and understanding in helping people to address their early experience.
- Be ready to accept that parents are likely to exert heavy demands on services and resources.
- Be ready to respond to early signs of stress instead of waiting for a crisis to occur.
- Beware of underestimating the contribution which practical supports can make to helping families under pressure.
- Explore practical ways of reducing the pressures on the family from environmental threats in order to lighten the parental load.
- How support is delivered matters as much as what support is delivered.
- Maintain continuity in service delivery.

- Maintain good inter-agency co-ordination and professional collaboration.
- Mobilize community supports and ensure close integration of formal services with informal networks.
- Periodic and ongoing long-term 'refresher' support is needed to maintain learned skills.
- Practitioners should have a genuine liking or feeling for families with which they are involved.
- The acquisition of new skills is more likely and training more effective where clearly specified, individualized goals are set and presented in small, discrete and concrete steps.
- Training is less effective where parents are having to cope with external pressures in their lives (such as debt, homelessness, harassment, the protective agencies, opposition from their extended family) and are preoccupied with the crises of day-to-day survival.
- Training must be geared to parental learning characteristics – for example, their slower rate of learning, inability to read, low self-esteem, difficulties in organizing, sequencing and sticking to time schedules, need for more intensive and continuous supervision – and a heavy initial investment in establishing trust and rapport will improve participation.
- Training tends to be more effective when it is intensive, consistent and continuous rather than irregular, infrequent and provided by different agencies or changing staff.

Rights and citizenship

- Ensure that parents have access to independent, informed and sympathetic advice whenever issues relating to parental responsibilities and child care arise.
- Never seek permanently to remove a child from home for reasons of neglect, inadequate care or abuse by omission before every effort has been made to equip the parents with the skills they need to cope.
- Parents should be enabled to participate in the making of decisions with a bearing on their family life or on the welfare of their children.
- Support tends to be most effective when it is consistent, non-intrusive and non-threatening.

Good parenting

- A parent–child relationship based on love and affection is more easily supported than replaced.

- Always bear in mind that the parent–child relationship may be worth supporting even when a parent cannot meet all the developmental needs of the child.
- Always ensure that people's parenting abilities and problems are assessed in the context of their own lives and experience.
- Assessing the quality of parenting or family life calls for close familiarity based on long-term involvement.
- Avoid making value-laden judgements about the adequacy of parenting on the basis of unfair comparisons with middle-class standards.
- Be wary of underestimating the importance of the role played by fathers or partners.
- Be alert to the possibly damaging effects of physical, sexual or system abuse on parents' own functioning.
- Do not adopt too narrow a view of the parenting task: there is more to parenting than merely practical skills.
- Ensure that parents are made aware of the standards by which they are being judged.
- Never assume that parenting deficits are irremediable.
- Pay equal regard to people's parenting skills as well as their deficits.
- Remember that parenting is about more than childrearing.
- Remember that the need for belonging on the part of children may outweigh any deficits observed in the competence of parents.
- Steer clear of self-fulfilling prophecies of parenting failure based on single-minded concern only with parental inadequacies.
- Training can improve the knowledge and skills of mothers and fathers in virtually all areas of parenting, although the extent of learning varies between individuals.

Social justice and discrimination

- Approach each case with an open mind; parental competence can only be assessed on a case-by-case basis.
- Avoid blaming the victim by ascribing poor childrearing to the limitations of the parents where it owes more to the constraints of their social situation.
- Avoid interfering in family matters that have no bearing on the reasons for intervention.
- Be careful not to make judgements about parents with learning difficulties as a group or class.
- Be wary of allowing gendered assumptions to bias the assessment of parental competence.
- Ensure that parents with learning difficulties are not treated more

punitively than other parents whose problems similarly stem from a disadvantaged upbringing.
● Practitioners must be aware of their capacity for exacerbating the stress on families and augmenting the problems they face.

Most current work with parents who have learning difficulties strays a long way from these guidelines. The personal stories we have recounted illustrate the gap that has to be bridged. Indeed, our study has shown that the problems encountered by parents are often made worse by the services provided for their support. A lot of the trouble comes from child protection workers who lack experience in the learning difficulties field and from unqualified support workers and social work assistants who, generally good-heartedly, allow moralistic, governessy, meddlesome instincts to intrude into their work. Yet even practitioners whose sympathies are with the parents can find themselves trapped by the system into taking actions or decisions that oppress them. For this reason, changing practice is not only about educating practitioners but also about changing the service system in which they must operate and attitudes within the wider society. From this point of view, these guidelines are not only a challenge to practitioners but also a challenge to ourselves.

References

Accardo, P. and Whitman, B. (1990) 'Children of mentally retarded parents', *American Journal of Diseases of Children*, 144, 69–70.

Allport, G. (1947) *The Use of Personal Documents in Psychological Science*. New York, Social Science Research Council.

Andron, L. and Sturm, M. (1973) 'Is "I do" in the repertoire of the retarded? A study of the functioning of married retarded couples', *Mental Retardation*, 11(1), 31–4.

Andron, L. and Tymchuk, A. (1987) 'Parents who are mentally retarded', in A. Craft (ed.) *Mental Handicap and Sexuality: Issues and Perspectives*. Tunbridge Wells, D.J. Costello.

Atkinson, D. (1988) 'Research interviews with people with mental handicaps', *Mental Handicap Research*, 1(1), 75–90.

Atkinson, D. and Williams, F. (eds) (1990) *Know Me As I Am – An Anthology of Prose, Poetry and Art by People with Learning Difficulties*. London, Hodder and Stoughton in association with Open University Press.

Attard, M. (1988) 'Mentally handicapped parents – some issues to consider in relation to pregnancy', *British Journal of Mental Subnormality*, 34(66), 3–9.

Bass, M. (1963–64) 'Marriage, parenthood and prevention of pregnancy', *American Journal of Mental Deficiency*, 39(11), 318–33.

Becker, H. (1967) 'Whose side are we on?', *Social Problems*, 14(3), 239–47.

Berg, E. and Nyland, D. (1975) 'Marriage and mental retardation in Denmark', in D. Primrose (ed.) *Proceedings of the Third Congress of the International Association for the Scientific Study of Mental Deficiency, Vol. I*. Warsaw, Polish Medical Publishers.

Berger, P. (1966) *Invitation to Sociology*. Harmondsworth, Penguin.

Bertaux, D. (1981) 'Introduction', in D. Bertaux (ed.) *Biography and Society*. London, Sage Publications.

Bertaux, D. and Bertaux-Wiame, I. (1981) 'Life stories in the bakers' trade', in D. Bertaux (ed.) *Biography and Society*. London, Sage Publications.

Bertaux, D. and Kohli, M. (1984) 'The life story approach: a continental view', *American Review of Sociology*, 10, 215–37.

Bertaux-Wiame, I. (1981) 'The life-history approach to the study of internal migration', in D. Bertaux (ed.) *Biography and Society*. London, Sage Publications.

Biklen, S. and Moseley, C. (1988) '"Are you retarded? No, I'm Catholic": qualitative methods in the study of people with severe handicaps', *Journal of the Association of Severe Handicaps*, 13(8), 155–62.

Birren, J. and Deutchman, D. (1991) *Guiding Autobiography Groups for Older Adults*. Baltimore, MD and London, Johns Hopkins University Press.

Birren, J. and Hedlund, B. (1987) 'Contributions of autobiography to developmental psychology', in N. Eisenberg (ed.) *Contemporary Topics in Developmental Psychology*. New York, John Wiley.

Bogdan, R. (1974) *Being Different: The Autobiography of Jane Fry*. New York, Wiley.

Bogdan, R. and Taylor, S. (1976) 'The judged, not the judges: an insider's view of mental retardation', *American Psychologist*, 31, 47–52.

Bogdan, R. and Taylor, S. (1982) *Inside Out: The Social Meaning of Retardation*. Toronto, University of Toronto Press.

Booth, T., Simons, K. and Booth W. (1990) *Outward Bound: Relocation and Community Care for People with Learning Difficulties*. Milton Keynes, Open University Press.

Booth, W. and Fielden, S. (1992) 'Second opinions: students' views of Swallow Street Centre'. Unpublished report, Department of Sociological Studies, University of Sheffield.

Bowker, G. (1993) 'The age of biography is upon us', *Times Higher Education Supplement*, 8 January, 19.

Brandon, D. and Ridley, J. (1983) *Beginning to Listen – A Study of the Views of Residents Living in a Hostel for Mentally Handicapped People*. London, MIND.

Brandon, M. (1957) 'The intellectual and social status of children of mental defectives', *Journal of Mental Science*, 103, 710–38.

Brandon, M. (1960) 'A survey of 200 women discharged from a mental deficiency hospital', *Journal of Mental Science*, 106, 355–70.

Brantlinger, E. (1988) 'Teachers' perceptions of the parenting abilities of their secondary students with mild mental retardation', *Remedial and Special Education*, 9(4), 31–43.

Budd, K. and Greenspan, S. (1984) 'Mentally retarded mothers', in E. Blechman (ed.) *Behavior Modification with Women*. New York, Guilford Press.

Budd, K. and Greenspan, S. (1985) 'Parameters of successful and unsuccessful intervention for parents who are mentally retarded', *Mental Retardation*, 23(6), 269–73.

Cattermole, M., Jahoda, A. and Markova, J. (1987) *Leaving Home: The Experience of People with a Mental Handicap*. Department of Psychology, University of Stirling.

Craft, A. (1993) 'Parents with learning disabilities – an overview', in A. Craft (ed.) *Parents with Learning Disabilities*. Kidderminster, BILD.

Crain, L. and Millor, G. (1978) 'Forgotten children: maltreated children of mentally retarded parents', *Pediatrics*, 61(1), 130–32.

Czukar, G. (1983) 'Legal aspects of parenthood for mentally retarded persons', *Canadian Journal of Community Mental Handicap*, 2, 57–69.

Denzin, N. (1970) *Sociological Methods: A Sourcebook*. London, Butterworth.

152   *Parenting under pressure*

Denzin, N. (1989) *Interpretive Biography*. London, Sage.

Donaldson, S. (1992) 'Support for parents with mental handicap'. Unpublished manuscript, Woodlands Hospital, Cults, Aberdeen.

Douglas, J. (1976) *Investigative Social Research: Individual and Team Field Research*. Beverley Hills, CA, Sage.

Dowdney, L. and Skuse, D. (1993) 'Parenting provided by adults with mental retardation', *Journal of Child Psychology and Psychiatry*, 34(1), 25–47.

Dowdney, L., Skuse, D., Rutter, M., Quinton, D. and Mrazek, D. (1985) 'The nature and quality of parenting provided by women raised in institutions', *Journal of Child Psychology and Psychiatry*, 26(4), 599–625.

Edgerton, R. (1967) *The Cloak of Competence: Stigma in the Lives of the Mentally Retarded*. Berkeley, University of California Press.

Edgerton, R., Bollinger, M. and Herr, B. (1984) 'The cloak of competence: after two decades', *American Journal of Mental Deficiency*, 88(4), 345–51.

Erikson, K. (1973) 'Sociology and the historical perspective', in M. Drake (ed.), *Applied Historical Studies*. London, Methuen in association with Open University Press.

Espe-Sherwindt, M. and Kerlin, S. (1990) 'Early intervention with parents with mental retardation: do we empower or impair?', *Infants and Young Children*, 2, 21–8.

Faraday, A. and Plummer, K. (1979) 'Doing life histories', *Sociological Review*, 27, November, 773–98.

Farmer, R., Rohde, J. and Sacks, B. (1993) *Changing Services for People with Learning Disabilities*. London, Chapman & Hall.

Feldman, M. (1986) 'Research on parenting by mentally retarded persons', *Psychiatric Clinics of North America*, 9(4), 777–96.

Feldman, M., Case, L., Towns, F. and Betel, J. (1985) 'Parent education project I: development and nurturance of children of mentally retarded parents', *American Journal of Mental Deficiency*, 90(3), 253–58.

Feldman, M., Towns, F., Betel, J., Case, L., Rincover, A. and Rubino, C. (1986) 'Parent education project II: increasing stimulating interactions of developmentally handicapped mothers', *Journal of Applied Behavior Analysis*, 19(1), 23–37.

Feldman, M., Case, L., Rincover, A., Towns, F. and Betel, J. (1989) 'Parent education project III: increasing affection and responsivity in developmentally handicapped mothers', *Journal of Applied Behavior Analysis*, 22(2), 211–22.

Ferrarotti, F. (1981) 'On the autonomy of the biographical method', in D. Bertaux (ed.), *Biography and Society*. London, Sage Publications.

Floor, L., Baxter, D., Rosen, M. and Zisfein, L. (1975) 'A survey of marriages among previously institutionalized retardates', *Mental Retardation*, 13(2), 33–7.

Flynn, M. (1986) 'Adults who are mentally handicapped as consumers: issues and guidelines for interviewing', *Journal of Mental Deficiency Research*, 30, 369–77.

Flynn, M. (1989) *Independent Living for Adults with Mental Handicap*, London, Cassell.

Fotheringham, J. (1980) 'Mentally retarded persons are parents'. Unpublished manuscript, Department of Psychiatry, Queen's University, Kingston, Ontario, Canada.

Fotheringham, J. (1981) 'Mild mental retardation, poverty and parenthood'. Unpublished manuscript, Department of Psychiatry, Queen's University, Kingston, Ontario, Canada.

Galliher, K. (1973) 'Termination of the parent/child relationship: should parental IQ be an important factor?', *Law and the Social Order*, 4, 855–79.

Gaston, C. (1982) 'The use of personal documents in the study of adulthood'. Paper presented at the annual meeting of the American Psychological Association, Washington, DC.

Gath, A. (1988) 'Mentally handicapped people as parents', *Journal of Child Psychology and Psychiatry*, 29(6), 739–44.

Gilhool, T. and Gran, J. (1985) 'Legal rights of disabled parents', in S. Thurman (ed.) *Children of Handicapped Parents: Research and Clinical Perspectives*. New York, Academic Press.

Gillberg, C. and Geijer-Karlsson, M. (1983) 'Children born to mentally retarded women: a 1–21 year follow-up study of 41 cases', *Psychological Medicine*, 13, 891–94.

Gittins, D. (1979) 'Oral history, reliability and recollection', in L. Moss and H. Goldstein (eds), *The Recall Method in Social Surveys*. London, University of London Institute of Education.

Glaser, B. and Strauss, A. (1967) *The Discovery of Grounded Theory*. Chicago, Aldine.

Greenspan, S. and Budd, K. (1986) 'Research on mentally retarded parents', in J. Gallagher and P. Vietze (eds) *Families of Handicapped Persons: Research Programmes and Policy Issues*. Baltimore, MD, Paul H. Brookes.

Haavik, S. and Menninger, K. (1981) *Sexuality, Law and the Developmentally Disabled Person: Legal and Clinical Aspects of Marriage, Parenthood, and Sterilization*. Baltimore, MD, Paul H. Brookes.

Harris, R. (1990) 'A matter of balance: power and resistance in child protection policy', *Journal of Social Welfare Law*, 5, 332–39.

Hayes, M. (1993) 'Child care law: An overview', in A. Craft (ed.) *Parents with Learning Disabilities*. Kidderminster, BILD.

Johnson, M. (1976) 'That was your life: a biographical approach to later life', in J. Munnichs and W. van den Heuvel (eds) *Dependency or Interdependency in Old Age*. The Hague, Martinus Nijhoff.

Johnson, P. and Clark, S. (1984) 'Service needs of developmentally disabled parents', in J. Berg and J. de Jong (eds) *Perspectives and Progress in Mental Retardation, Vol. 1*. Baltimore, MD, University Park Press.

Kaminer, R., Jedrysek, E. and Soles, B. (1981) 'Intellectually limited parents', *Journal of Developmental and Behavioral Pediatrics*, 2(2), 39–43.

King's Fund Centre (1980) *An Ordinary Life: Comprehensive Locally-based Residential Services for Mentally Handicapped People*. London, King's Fund Centre.

Kohli, M. (1981) 'Biography: account, text and method', in D. Bertaux (ed.) *Biography and Society*. London, Sage Publications.

Laxova, R., Gilderdale, S. and Ridler, M. (1973) 'An aetiological study of 53 female patients from a subnormality hospital and their offspring', *Journal of Mental Deficiency Research*, 17, 193–216.

154   *Parenting under pressure*

Lazarus, R. (1966) *Psychological Stress and the Coping Process*. New York, McGraw-Hill.

Llewellyn, G. (1990) 'People with intellectual disability as parents: perspectives from the professional literature', *Australian and New Zealand Journal of Developmental Disabilities*, 16(4), 369–80.

Llewellyn, G. (1991) 'Parents with intellectual disability: parent and professional perspectives'. Paper presented at the IASSMD International Conference on Mental Retardation, Hong Kong, March.

Local Government Ombudsman (1991) *Investigation into Complaint No. 89/C/2577 against Lancashire County Council*, 17 December. York, Commission for Local Administration in England.

Lowe, K., de Paiva, S. and Humphreys, S. (1986) *Long Term Evaluations of Services for People with a Mental Handicap in Cardiff: Clients' Views*. Cardiff, Mental Handicap in Wales, Applied Research Unit.

Lynch, E. and Bakley, S. (1989) 'Serving young children whose parents are mentally retarded', *Infants and Young Children*, 1, 26–38.

Madsen, M. (1979) 'Parenting classes for the mentally retarded', *Mental Retardation*, 17, August, 195–96.

Malin, N. (1983) *Group Homes for Mentally Handicapped People*. London, HMSO.

McConachie, H. (1991) 'Families and professionals: prospects for partnership', in S. Segal and V. Varma (eds) *Prospects for People with Learning Difficulties*. London, David Fulton Publishers.

McGaw, S. (1993) 'Working with parents on parenting skills', in A. Craft (ed.) *Parents with Learning Disabilities*. Kidderminster, BILD.

Mercer, J. (1973) *Labelling the Mentally Retarded: Clinical and Social System Perspectives on Mental Retardation*. Berkeley and London, University of California Press.

Mickelson, P. (1947) 'The feebleminded parent: a study of 90 family cases', *American Journal of Mental Deficiency*, 51, 644–45.

Mickelson, P. (1949) 'Can mentally deficient parents be helped to give their children better care?', *American Journal of Mental Deficiency*, 53(3), 516–34.

Miller, W. (1981) 'A special problem in primary prevention: the family that cares about their children but is not able to rear them', *Journal of Clinical Child Psychology*, Winter, 38–41.

Mira, M. and Roddy, J. (1980) 'Parenting competencies of retarded persons: a critical review'. Unpublished manuscript, Children's Rehabilitation Unit, University of Kansas Medical Center.

Mount, B. and Zwernik, K. (1988) *It's Never Too Early, It's Never Too Late: A Booklet about Personal Futures Planning*. Publication no. 421–88–109, Metropolitan Council, St Paul, Minnesota.

O'Brien, J. (1987) *Learning from Citizen Advocacy Programs*. Georgia Advocacy Office, Atlanta.

Painz, F. (1993) *Parents with a Learning Disability*. Social Work Monographs no. 116, University of East Anglia, Norwich.

Parkes, M. (1971) 'Psycho-social transitions: a field for study', *Social Science and Medicine*, 5(2), 101–15.

Passfield, D. (1983) 'What do you think of it so far? A survey of 20 Priory Court residents', *Mental Handicap*, 11(3), 97–99.

Payne, A. (1978) 'The law and the problem parent: custody and parental rights of homosexual, mentally retarded, mentally ill and incarcerated parents', *Journal of Family Law*, 16, 797–818.

Penrose, L. (1938) 'Colchester survey – a clinical and genetic study of 1280 cases of mental defect', *Special Report Senior Medical Council*, no. 229. London, HMSO.

People First of Washington, (1985) *Speaking Up and Speaking Out*. A Report on the International Self-Advocacy Leadership Conference, July 23–29, 1984. People First of Washington and University of Oregon.

Perrin, B. and Nirje, B. (1985) 'Setting the record straight: a critique of some frequent misconceptions of the normalization principle', *Australia and New Zealand Journal of Developmental Disabilities*, 11(2), 69–74.

Petchesky, R. (1979) 'Reproduction, ethics, and public policy: the federal sterilization regulations', *The Hastings Center*, October, 29–41.

Peterson, S., Robinson, E. and Littman, I. (1983) 'Parent–child interaction training for parents with a history of mental retardation', *Applied Research in Mental Retardation*, 4, 329–42.

Phillips, D. (1971) *Knowledge from What? Theories and Methods in Social Research*. Chicago, Rand McNally.

Plummer, K. (1983) *Documents of Life*. London, Allen & Unwin.

Potts, M. and Fido, R. (1990) *They Take My Character*. Plymouth, Northcote House.

Prosser, J. (1992) *Child Abuse Investigations: The Families' Perspective*. Stansted, Essex, Parents Against INjustice (PAIN).

Quinton, D. and Rutter, M. (1984a) 'Parents with children in care – I. Current circumstances and parenting skills', *Journal of Child Psychology and Psychiatry*, 25, 211–29.

Quinton, D. and Rutter, M. (1984b) 'Parents with children in care – II. Intergenerational continuities', *Journal of Child Psychology and Psychiatry*, 25, 231–50.

Quinton, D., Rutter, M. and Liddle, C. (1984) 'Institutional rearing, parenting difficulties and marital support', *Psychological Medicine*, 14, 107–24.

Richards, S. (1984) *Community Care of the Mentally Handicapped: Consumer Perspectives*. University of Birmingham.

Richardson, A. and Ritchie, J. (1989) *Developing Friendships: Enabling People with Learning Difficulties to Make and Maintain Friends*. London, Policy Studies Institute.

Rosenburg, S. and McTate, G. (1982) 'Intellectually handicapped mothers: problems and prospects', *Children Today*, 37, January/February, 24–26

Scally, B. (1973) 'Marriage and mental handicap: some observations in Northern Ireland', in F. de la Cruz and G. LaVeck (eds) *Human Sexuality and the Mentally Retarded*. New York, Brunner/Mazel.

Schilling, R., Schinke, S., Blythe, B. and Barth, R. (1982) 'Child maltreatment and mentally retarded parents: is there a relationship?', *Mental Retardation*, 20(5), 201–09.

Seagull, E. and Scheurer, S. (1986) 'Neglected and abused children of mentally retarded parents', *Child Abuse and Neglect*, 10(4), 493–500.

Shaw, C. and Wright, C. (1960) 'The married mental defective: a follow-up study', *The Lancet*, 30 January, 273–74.

Sigelman, C., Schoenrock, C., Winer, J., Spanhel, C., Hromas, S., Martin, P., Budd, E. and Bensberg, C. (1981a) 'Issues in interviewing mentally retarded persons: an empirical study', in R. Bruininks, C. Meyer, B. Sigford and K. Lakin (eds) *Deinstitutionalization and Community Adjustment of Mentally Retarded People*, Monograph No. 4. American Association of Mental Deficiency, Washington, DC.

Sigelman, C., Budd, E., Spanhel, C. and Schoenrock, C. (1981b) 'When in doubt, say yes: acquiescence in interviews with mentally retarded persons', *Mental Retardation*, April, 53–58.

Sigelman, C., Budd, E., Winer, J., Schoenrock, C. and Martin, P. (1982) 'Evaluating alternative techniques of questioning mentally retarded persons', *American Journal of Mental Deficiency*, 86(5), 511–18.

Sugg, B. (1987) 'Community care: the consumer's point of view', *Community Care*, 645, 22 January, 6.

Thompson, A. (1984) 'The assessment and remediation through play therapy of parenting competencies of mentally retarded mothers', *Dissertation Abstracts International*, 45, 01, July, 379.

Thompson, P. (1981) 'Life histories and the analysis of social change', in D. Bertaux (ed.) *Biography and Society*. London, Sage Publications.

Thompson, P. (1992) ' "I don't feel old": subjective ageing and the search for meaning in later life', *Ageing and Society*, 12, 23–47.

Towell, D. (1982) 'Foreword – progress towards "An Ordinary Life" ', in King's Fund Centre, *An Ordinary Life*. London, King's Fund Centre.

Tremblay, M. (1957) 'The key informant technique: a non-ethnographic application', *American Anthropologist*, 59, 688–98.

Tucker, M. and Johnson, O. (1989) 'Competence promoting vs. competence inhibiting social support for mentally retarded mothers', *Human Organisation*, 48(2), 95–107.

Turk, V. and Brown, H. (1992) 'Sexual abuse and adults with learning disabilities', *Mental Handicap*, 20(2), 56–58.

Tymchuk, A. (1990a) 'Assessing emergency responses of people with mental handicaps: an assessment instrument', *Mental Handicap*, 18(4), 136–42.

Tymchuk, A. (1990b) *Parents with Mental Retardation: A National Strategy*. Paper prepared for the President's Committee on Mental Retardation, SHARE/UCLA Parenting Project, Department of Psychiatry, School of Medicine, University of California at Los Angeles.

Tymchuk, A. (1992) 'Predicting adequacy of parenting by people with mental retardation', *Child Abuse and Neglect*, 16(2), 165–78.

Tymchuk, A., Andron, L. and Rahbar, B. (1988) 'Effective decision-making/problem-solving training with mothers who have mental retardation', *American Journal of Mental Retardation*, 92(6), 510–16.

Tymchuk, A., Andron, L. and Tymchuk, M. (1990) 'Training mothers with mental handicaps to understand behavioural and developmental principles', *Mental Handicap Research*, 3, 51–59.

Tymchuk, A., Andron, L. and Ungar, O. (1987) 'Parents with mental handicaps and adequate child care – a review', *Mental Handicap*, 15, June, 49–54.

Tymchuk, A. and Feldman, M. (1991) 'Parents with mental retardation and their children: review of research relevant to professional practice', *Canadian Psychology*, 32(3), 486–96.

Tymchuk, A. and Keltner, B. (n.d.) *Advantage Profiles: A Tool for Health Care Professionals Working with Parents with Mental Retardation*, SHARE/UCLA Parenting Project, Department of Psychiatry, School of Medicine, University of California at Los Angeles.

Unger, O. and Howes, C. (1986) 'Mother–child interactions and symbolic play between toddlers and their adolescent or mentally retarded mothers', *Occupational Therapy Journal of Research*, 8(4), 237–49.

Walton-Allen, N. and Feldman, M. (1991) 'Perception of service needs by parents who are mentally retarded and their social service workers', *Comprehensive Mental Health Care*, 1(2), 137–47.

Welsh Office. (1991a) *The Review of the All Wales Strategy: A View from the Carers*. Cardiff, Social Services Inspectorate.

Welsh Office. (1991b) *The Review of the All Wales Strategy: A View from the Staff*. Cardiff, Social Services Inspectorate.

Welsh Office. (1991c) *The Review of the All Wales Strategy: A View from the Users*. Cardiff, Social Services Inspectorate.

Whitman, B. and Accardo, P. (eds.) (1990) *When a Parent Is Mentally Retarded*. Baltimore, MD, Paul H. Brookes.

Whitman, B., Graves, B. and Accardo, P. (1986) 'The mentally retarded parent in the community: an epidemiological study', *Developmental Medicine and Child Neurology*, supplement, 53, 18.

Whitman, B., Graves, B. and Accardo, P. (1989) 'Training in parenting skills for adults with mental retardation', *Social Work*, 34(5), 431–34.

Whitman, B., Graves, B. and Accardo, P. (1990) 'Parents learning together I: parenting skills training for adults with mental retardation', in B. Whitman and P. Accardo (eds) *When a Parent Is Mentally Retarded*. Baltimore, MD, Paul H. Brookes.

Wunsch, W. (1951) 'The first complete tabulation of the Rhode Island Mental Deficiency Register', *American Journal of Mental Deficiency*, 55, 293–312.

Wyngaarden, M. (1981) 'Interviewing mentally retarded persons: issues and strategies', in R. Bruininks, C. Meyer, B. Sigford and K. Lakin (eds) *Deinstitutionalization and Community Adjustment of Mentally Retarded People*, Monograph No. 4. American Association of Mental Deficiency, Washington, DC.

Young, J. (1969) 'The zoo-keepers of deviancy', *Anarchy*, 98, April, 38–46.

Zetlin, A., Weisner T. and Gallimore, R. (1985) 'Diversity, shared functioning, and the role of benefactors: a study of parenting by retarded persons', in S. Thurman (ed.) *Children of Handicapped Parents: Research and Clinical Perspectives*. New York, Academic Press.

CARERS PERCEIVED
POLICY AND PRACTICE IN INFORMAL CARE

Julia Twigg and Karl Atkin

Carers are the bedrock of community care, and yet our understanding of how they do and do not fit into the care system is limited. Concern is often expressed about the need to support carers, but the best way to do this is not always clear.

This book breaks new ground in exploring the reality of how service providers like doctors, social workers, and community nurses respond to carers. It looks at which carers get help and why, analysing how age, relationship, class and gender structure the responses of service providers and carers. It examines the moral and policy issues posed by trying to incorporate carers' interests into service provision. What would services look like if they took the needs of carers seriously? How far can they afford to do so? Is this only achieved at the expense of disabled people? What is the proper relationship between carers and services? Carers pose in acute form many of the central dilemmas of social welfare, and the account presented here has the widest significance for the analysis of community care.

Focusing on the views of carers as well as service providers, the book looks at caring across a variety of relationships and conditions, including people with mental health problems and learning disabilities.

Contents
Informal care – Carers in the service system – The carers' experience – Social services – The health sector – Services in a mixed setting – Carers of people with learning disabilities – Carers of adults with mental health problems – Mediating – Structuring – Carers in the policy arena – Appendix – References – Index.

192pp   0 335 19111 8 (Paperback)   0 335 19112 6 (Hardback)

COORDINATING COMMUNITY CARE
MULTIDISCIPLINARY TEAMS AND CARE MANAGEMENT

John Øvretveit

This book is about how people from different professions and agencies work together to meet the health and social needs of people in a community. It is about making the most of different skills to meet people's needs, and creating satisfying and supportive working groups. It is about the details of making community care a reality.

The effectiveness and quality of care a person receives depends on getting the right professionals and services, and also on the support given to the person's carers. Services must be coordinated if the person is to benefit, but coordination is more difficult with the increasing change, variety and complexity of health and social services in the 1990s. This book challenges the assumptions that services are best coordinated by multi-professional and multi-agency teams, and that community care teams are broadly similar. It demonstrates when a team is needed and how to overcome differences between professions, and between agency policies and philosophies.

Drawing on ten years of consultancy research with a variety of teams and services, the author gives practical guidance for managers and practitioners about how to set up and improve coordination and teamwork. The book combines practical concerns with theoretical depth drawing on organization and management theory, psychology, psychoanalysis, sociology, economics and government studies.

Contents
Introduction – Needs and organization – Markets, bureaucracy and association – Types of team – Client pathways and team resource management – Team members' roles – Team leadership – Decisions and conflict in teams – Communications and co-service – Coordinating community health and social care – Appendices – Glossary – References and bibliography – Index.

240pp   0 335 19047 2 (Paperback)   0 335 19048 0 (Hardback)

OUTWARD BOUND
RELOCATION AND COMMUNITY CARE FOR PEOPLE WITH LEARNING
DIFFICULTIES

Tim Booth, Ken Simons and Wendy Booth

Current mental handicap policies aim to bring about a shift in responsibility and resources for residential care from large institutions to small homely units. In practice this means closing long-stay wards or complete hospitals and moving the patients out into the community. This book examines the outcome of one such community care programme through the views and feelings of staff, families and the movers involved. It explores the experiences of two groups of people, one of which moved out of long-stay hospitals to take up places in locally based hostels, while the other moved out of hostels into independent living accommodation in the community. Based on the findings of a three year research project funded by the Joseph Rowntree Foundation, the book addresses the personal issues and the policy implications of relocating people with learning difficulties in line with the government's plans for community care.

Contents
The policy context – Ways and means: the study design – Out of step: issues of process and adjustment – Handling the move – New homes for old? – View from the office – Learning to listen – Speaking for ourselves – Relatively speaking – From all sides now: the changes in perspective – Last words – Bibliography – Index.

208pp   0 335 15430 1 (Paperback)   0 335 15431 X (Hardback)